Not Just Yes and Amen

CHRISTIANS WITH A CAUSE

Dorothee Soelle *and* Fulbert Steffensky

FORTRESS PRESS

PHILADELPHIA

———————

Library of Congress Cataloging in Publication Data

Sölle, Dorothee.
  Not just yes and amen.

  Translation of: Nicht nur ja und amen.
  1. Christian life—1960– . 2. Theology,
Doctrinal—Popular works. 3. Apologetics—20th century.
I. Steffensky, Fulbert. II. Title.
BV4501.2.S636 1985   230   84–48708
ISBN 0–8006–1828–9

———————

1249K84   Printed in the United States of America   1–1828

Contents

Introduction   5

Justice: A Feeling of Rage in the Pit of Your Stomach   8

Sin: Where Is Your Brother? Where Is Your Sister?   14

Grace: The Best Thing in Life Really Is Free   19

Miracle: The Lame Walk   23

Creation: Behold, It Was All Very Good   28

Freedom: No One Is Powerless   34

Prayer: Learning What We Really Want   38

Discipleship: What You Really Want to Do with Your Life   43

Faith: All Things Are Possible   51

Church: They Had Everything in Common   57

Eternal Life: To Remain in Love   64

Kingdom of God: Freedom from Having, Freedom for Living   68

Cross: The Cry of the Tortured   73

Contents

God: Nothing Is Lost   79

Resurrection: Mystery of Faith   83

Peace: God Disarms Unilaterally   87

Introduction

Let's be candid about one thing: the coauthors of this book—Fulbert and Dorothee, married, four children—are Christians, and we are not writing from a distance as if we were detached observers. We feel ourselves bound to Jesus and therefore have named ourselves after him. We are "Christians," people who belong to Christ. At least we try to be Christians. Not because our parents once had us baptized, and not because we want to pass on a tradition like a neatly wrapped-up package, but because we think that it is better to be with Jesus than to be without him. That means that we are seeking a life different from the one we now have, and we know that Jesus helps us by showing us the way, by making us freer and happier and also a little better than we are right now. Therefore we need religion, and the best one that we have been able to discover is the Christian religion. Lots of people will argue with that, but maybe they will read through this book first to hear our reasons for saying so.

While riding recently on a train, I was sitting next to a matronly woman who wondered why I was reading so intently. She finally began to quiz me a little about where I was going and where I was from and what I did for a living. I didn't know what I should say: "What I do for a living?—Well, uh—I do theology," I finally muttered.

"What?" she replied. "Theology?"

"Right," I said, somewhat embarrassed, "you know . . . religion."

"Are you a pastor then?" she asked.

"Well, kind of," I replied. "I write books about religion."

We need to stop and ask why such an exchange is so painful, why it brings us to stuttering. It has something to do with the church. That we are interested in Jesus, that we like to sing hymns old and new, that we hold the Bible to be one of the best books ever written—these are things we certainly don't need to be ashamed of. The problem is the church! Most people we know think of the church as boring, naive, superficial, maybe something for the old and the sick, but not for them. Well, we can't simply be "yes-people" for the church. We are embarrassed on account of the church. It's like we come from a lousy family: father drinks, mother yells, and the kids fight the whole day. Bishops drive limousines to hunger conferences, only a few old women ever come to church, and the kids are happy when they can pocket their confirmation money. Some kind of family.

Funny thing is, it's *our* family, in spite of it all. We find it to be unbearable, stupid, next to impossible, phony—but we still stay with it. Instead of dropping out, we stick all the more to it. In other words we say: Dad drinks, and Mom yells . . . but Grandma is super and my little brother is absolutely the greatest. That's the way it is with the church, at least with both of the large German churches,* whose differences we find so insignificant. The church leadership and the bishops have developed into a real art the ability to say neither yes nor no. For example, to the question of whether they would rather have more or fewer atomic bombs, most of the time they say "yo," yes and no. Clergy talk too much, church members have been asleep for centuries . . . but Jesus simply can't be done away with, and there isn't much to be said against people like Albert Schweitzer and Dietrich Bonhoeffer and Martin Luther King, Jr.

It is these people—and God knows they are not just people who say yes and amen to everything—that we want to think about in this book. We want to talk about them. We want to try to say what it is that we find good about religion, why we need God and Christ and the Spirit, and why we put up with the church.

We don't want to be counted among those who simply avoid thinking seriously and who swallow everything and never question what they are told; who go along with something when they themselves don't really believe it; who participate half the time and the rest of the

*By "both" German churches the authors are referring to the Protestant and the Roman Catholic churches in Germany.

time laugh at others who have the same wishy-washy position. So first we want to explain what religion is *not*. It is not:

1. something to be learned by rote memorization, by which we gain Brownie points for repeating the right words and phrases;
2. a feeling that we can pull out of the closet once or twice a year, when it's time for Christmas or a funeral;
3. an institution that thinks everyone is so ignorant that they must be told whom they must vote for and which newspapers they should read;
4. a dogmatic code that tells people the things which come from above—from the government, the police, the school administration, the nuclear plants, and the military—and which things are good and right to believe.

All this is not religion, but rather a curious mixture of ignorance, obedience, insensitivity, mental paralysis, and cowardice, with a mild infusion about God thrown in. Real religion, that is, when it is genuinely practiced, is totally another thing. A true Christian has doubts about his or her faith, as well as the difficulties that go with believing; with the church and its representatives; with the Bible and its interpreters; with Jesus and what has been made of him; with God—and we don't even know whether we should call God *he* or *she*.

By far, the worst difficulties for the practicing Christian do not come from within the church, but, at least for us here in Germany, from the country in which we live because it is a very wealthy country in which God is seen as finally rubbish.

Jesus says: "I am the way, the truth, and the life" (John 14:6). He does not say: I am your happiness drug, I am the best computer, and I give you health forever. To that Way of which he speaks belong people who actually follow it; to that Truth which he means belong people who actually seek it; to that Life which he tells of belongs a question like: *Is it lived already*?

Come along, says this Jesus. Don't let anyone tell you that you will be happy if you live for money. God has much more in store for you than that.

Justice: A Feeling of Rage in the Pit of Your Stomach

One time when I was a child I saw three big guys jump a smaller boy, throw him to the ground, and beat him to a pulp. The little kid yelled and screamed for mercy. I had a helpless feeling inside, a feeling of rage in the pit of my stomach. What could I do? They paid no attention to me, since I was even littler than my classmate. I screamed too, out of anger, out of revulsion, out of rage.

You have no doubt also experienced something like that. An example of injustice took place before your very eyes: someone bigger attacks someone smaller, strong attacks weak, or someone very shrewd and clever takes advantage of some slower person.

Someone owns a house and lets it stand empty. Eight other people live next door in three tiny, cramped rooms. Something is wrong here and we know it: it isn't fair! It shouldn't be allowed! A human being is not something that is there for other human beings to beat up on and insult, to deceive and exploit, to cheat and ridicule.

Does this feeling of rage in the pit of your stomach have something to do with God? In every human being there is a need for justice, a feeling about justice, and a knowledge of what is unjust and unacceptable. Without justice we wouldn't be able to live. It is a natural thing to be upset over injustice. Many farmers and workers in the Third World would rather fight, offering what little possessions they have for what they consider to be just.

If we wish to speak about God, we must first know something about justice. First we must acquaint ourselves with that inner feeling of rage and anger over being too little, too weak, and too few to prevent what happens in various forms before our very eyes. That something like that should be possible! Most children are aware of this rage, but in the course of their lives it somehow gets lost or becomes dulled. To grow up then means to stamp out this inner sensitivity for justice. If you listen carefully within you for it, you will discover this sensitivity for justice. Then you will know: things simply can't continue the way they are! It's got to stop! You will then discover a power within yourself that says no to injustice and that wants to protect life. It may be the life of your grandmother that you would like to protect, or of a family from another country living next door, or even of a small animal that you know of. This power that makes us want to defend life, this love for justice, comes from God. To know God means to do what is just.

Lots of people talk about God in order to avoid this simple issue of justice by superpiously relating it to things outside this world. But we really can't know very much about God—apart from the issue of justice. We don't know where he lives: in heaven? next to the space capsules? We don't know what he looks like: is he white? And what would a person with black skin, whose great-grandparents were sold by whites as slaves, think about that? Could he or she think of God as having the same skin color as the slave dealer? We get into some problems when we start asking what God really looks like. Is he a man? Many people can't conceive of him otherwise. But more and more women today think that God could just as well be a woman as a man. And when you think of a woman who every evening is slapped around by her drunken husband, then it might dawn on us that God has to be a bit more than a man.

We can speculate all we want, but that doesn't add very much to what we really know about God. But there are two things that we are able to know about God: the first is that he knows us, and he knows us very well. Better, in fact, than all other people know us, and even better than we know ourselves. It is impossible to deceive him. It is possible to forget him. When we have silenced that sense of justice which dwells inside us, then we have forgotten God.

The second thing that we can determine about God is that we know what he wants from us: justice. If we're looking for a name for God, it might as well be the name "Justice." The Bible is very consistent on this point. It says that God is with us when we act justly. And when we are weak, small, unskilled, or disabled, we are with God together and are therefore stronger when we seek justice. When we live unjustly or keep our eyes and ears shut so that we do not have to take evil seriously, then God is far from us and foreign to us.

God calls one who acts unjustly to accountability. It is not true that injustice—like, for example, the arms race, which causes other people to suffer economic need and starvation—should always be seen as legitimate while never changing anything. God stands on the side of the disadvantaged and remains with them. He whispers in their ear that things are not always going to be the way they are right now. The Bible is a political book, a book that deals with justice and injustice. Let's not swallow the humbug that the Bible is *only* religious or that it is *purely religious*, because that is the invention of those who do not want to understand that God is Justice and that what God expects from us is something very concrete. There is a biblical story about a king and poor farmer in which something rather brutal happens.

Now Naboth the Jezreelite had a vineyard in Jezreel, beside the palace of Ahab king of Samaria. And after this Ahab said to Naboth, "Give me your vineyard, that I may have it for a vegetable garden, because it is near my house; and I will give you a better vineyard for it; or, if it seems good to you, I will give you its value in money." But Naboth said to Ahab, "The Lord forbid that I should give you the inheritance of my fathers." And Ahab went into his house vexed and sullen because of what Naboth the Jezreelite had said to him, for he had said, "I will not give you the inheritance of my fathers." And he lay down on his bed, and turned away his face, and would eat no food.

But Jezebel his wife came to him, and said to him, "Why is your spirit so vexed that you eat no food?" And he said to her, "Because I spoke to Naboth the Jezreelite, and said to him, 'Give me your vineyard for money; or else, if it please you, I will give you another vineyard for it; and he answered, 'I will not give you my vineyard.'" And Jezebel his wife said to him, "Do you now govern Israel? Arise, and eat bread, and let your heart be cheerful; I will give you the vineyard of Naboth the Jezreelite."

So she wrote letters in Ahab's name and sealed them with his seal, and she sent the letters to the elders and the nobles who dwelt with Naboth in his city. And she wrote in the letters, "Proclaim a fast, and set Naboth on high among the people; and set two base fellows opposite him, and let them bring a charge against him, saying, 'You have cursed God and the king.' Then take him out, and stone him to death." And the men of his city, the elders and the nobles who dwelt in his city, did as Jezebel had sent word to them. As it was written in the letters which she had sent to them, they proclaimed a fast, and set Naboth on high among the people. And the two base fellows came in and sat opposite him; and the base fellows brought a charge against Naboth, in the presence of the people, saying, "Naboth cursed God and the king." So they took him outside the city, and stoned him to death with stones. Then they sent to Jezebel, saying, "Naboth has been stoned; he is dead."

As soon as Jezebel heard that Naboth had been stoned and was dead, Jezebel said to Ahab, "Arise, take possession of the vineyard of Naboth the Jezreelite, which he refused to give you for money; for Naboth is not alive, but dead." And as soon as Ahab heard that Naboth was dead, Ahab arose to go down to the vineyard of Naboth the Jezreelite to take possession of it.

1 Kings 21:1–16

In our opinion the one who wrote this story must have known that inner feeling of rage we've been speaking about. Otherwise he couldn't have written it as he did. We know of other similar stories: a government devises a plan to clear some open fields in order to build a highway or an airport runway and offers a good price for the land. But the farmers resist the plan and try to prevent it. An open hearing is held and witnesses step forward. The authorities cite an old law that says a person can be prosecuted for speaking against *God and the king*.

When Queen Jezebel and her cronies use the word "God" they mean something quite different from the way we use it in this book. They mean a god who sides with the rich and powerful and who destroys the rights of the economically weak. "God" is used by Jezebel in order to stage a legal murder. The lawful power—namely, the law and the state authorities directed here by the queen—and the church join together in this action, so that a completely innocent person is murdered. King Ahab then takes over the vineyard.

Does the story stop here? The terrible thing is that we hear stories every day that stop here. Greed triumphs. The landlord raises the rent and kicks the old tenants out. The young teacher who has worked too openly for peace is not appointed to a teaching position. In Germany as well there are people of whom it is immediately said that they have a negative or an adversarial attitude toward God and

11

the government, especially if they are communists, for example. They then lose their jobs and join the ranks of the unemployed.

Many people then say: that's the way it goes. Can't do much about that. Whether the emperor, Hitler, Stalin—it's always the same. Whoever has the power also has all the rights. The rest should just accept that and never get involved.

But the stories of the Bible do not simply stop right here. Never, if you think about it. The important thing in this story is that they are speaking out against injustice. You can't break or bend what is truly lawful without being punished. Even when it looks like Naboth is dead and the king is the happy victor—the story is not at an end. God still has something to say. He surfaces in people who do not say: that's the way it is, has been, and always will be.

Speaking out is something that we can learn from the Bible, instead of just saying yes and amen to everything.

In our story God chooses a man named Elijah, who greets King Ahab with the words: "Thus says the Lord: 'Have you killed, and also taken possession?'" (1 Kings 21:19). To speak the truth to the powerful is an old tradition of the prophets. Among the Quakers in North America it belonged to the nature of being Christians to *speak truth to power.* That means: to discover the truth and not to act as if one saw and heard nothing. And speak the truth loudly! In the Bible the people who do this are called *prophets*. Their task is not to *foretell* something like a weather forecaster, but to offer to a people, a king, or a group of people the threat of punishment: this will happen to you if you continue on your present course. When the prophet Elijah spoke to Ahab, the king repented of what he had done. He mourned and fasted and changed.

The Bible doesn't simply let injustice stand. That would mean that God remains speechless. But God speaks—in small shepherd boys and in old women and in many others who on the outside don't look very noticeable. God speaks through them.

During the Nazi period many Jews in Germany had to flee the country and leave their homes behind. If they were able to sell their homes they received at best a ridiculously low price for them. Many Germans were happy to pick up a cheap Jewish villa. A young teacher came to the area where I grew up and was offered an empty house for a very cheap price. But he said: "I can't move into such a house. Legally and morally it still belongs to its former owner."

With that the young teacher made himself disliked by the Nazis. Everyone knew where he stood politically—just as we can know today where a teacher stands politically and whether he or she is for or against the military arms buildup. Back then it was much easier to find out. The young teacher was shortly afterward sent into a concentration camp.

Sin: Where Is Your Brother?
Where Is Your Sister?

We found the following notice in the newspaper and were pleased
that Isolde and Burkhard Bartel placed it there. We think it is right
that children like Saskia and Maren are growing up in a home environment in which the most important things are being discussed.

DEATH NOTICE

Of the 120 million children born in 1979, the year of the child, more
than 16 million have experienced hunger.

Today, Nov. 13, 1981, on the first day of Peace Week,

15,000 HUMAN BEINGS

are dying of hunger.

And on this day the rest of us are spending 1.4 billion dollars for
military weapons.

We are grieving,

Isolde and Burkhard Bartel
with Saskia (2¹/₂ yrs. old) and Maren (1)

The most important things as well as the most horrible things that
are happening in our century can be gathered from this notice in the
newspaper. Most people know—at least partially—how as adults we
come to learn many things. Our politicians know, yet most of them
think they must continue the arms buildup, produce more bombs,
and allow even more people to be victims of hunger.

We live in an economic system that sees to it that people in the
Third World are not healed of diseases we could have conquered long
ago. Because of malnutrition, especially lack of protein, more and
more children are suffering mental retardation. There are no schools

14

for them. Young girls sell themselves as prostitutes in order to feed their families.

What can we do? Does all this have anything to do with us? The Christian answer to this question is clear—even if we don't hear it often and clearly enough in the churches. The hunger of two-thirds of humanity is not the problem of those people who have too many children. It is our problem. We share the responsibility.

That feeling of rage in the pit of our stomach, the desire for justice, is now directed against two fronts. First of all, it is directed against those who can accept the notion of starving children and at the same time convince us with clever words of the necessity of more bombs. But our rage must also be directed against us, for when some of the family members suffer, then it should also concern those who have it good, normally the prosperous. That inner feeling of rage is not just a powerless feeling to be directed against the politicians who govern, but it also realizes that we are involved, and as long as we are willing to put up with what is happening, that inner feeling of rage is directed also against us.

When we were children the Nazis tried to exterminate Jews and Russians. These crimes were committed in the name of the German nation. We in Germany who were youths at the time belonged to this nation, and also those who were born much later belong to this same German nation. In this sense there is a sharing of responsibility as well as a sharing of guilt.

The injustice that is happening today is being planned by the white, wealthy nations of the world, to which we belong. In their trade agreements the rich countries are making sure that the poor become even poorer and are paid less and less for their raw materials and produce.

To give just one example: in 1972 one barrel of oil (= 40 gallons) cost 26 kilograms (57 lbs.) of bananas in the Third World. Today for the same amount of oil a banana grower has to pay 200 kilograms (almost 440 lbs.) of bananas. It keeps on going like this—and we are not at all innocent. We allow it to happen. Such a situation is what makes us say that in our country today God is seen finally as rubbish.

There is a connection between the hunger of some and the profit of others—and the Bible knows a great deal about this connection:

Not Just Yes and Amen

Her princes in the midst of her are like a roaring lion tearing the prey; they have devoured human lives; they have taken treasure and precious things; they have made many widows in the midst of her.

Ezekiel 22:25

The Bible has a special word for this involvement in exploitation: it is called *sin*, a word meaning to *sunder*, to *separate*. Sin is that which separates us from God. Even if we have inherited it from others there is still guilt because of the fact that we live in a world which is separated from God and in which there is so much hunger—when there doesn't have to be hunger at all. Guilt separates us from God, separates us from authentic living. God has no role any longer in our lives. When we store up more and more bombs and poison gas in our country, we do that against God. First of all, because we are planning and preparing for the deaths of other people (the Russians, for example), and second, because we are allowing the wasting away of human beings in the Third World, like the death notices constantly tell us.

The Bible holds no illusions over the fact that human beings kill each other, which happens seldom among animals of the same species. Envy and hatred toward those who are different from us are behind the feeling that we all have had from time to time: I could kill that person!

Now Adam knew Eve his wife, and she conceived and bore Cain, saying, "I have gotten a man with the help of the Lord." And again, she bore his brother Abel. Now Abel was a keeper of sheep, and Cain a tiller of the ground. In the course of time Cain brought to the Lord an offering of the fruit of the ground, and Abel brought of the firstlings of his flock and of their fat portions. And the Lord had regard for Abel and his offering, but for Cain and his offering he had no regard. So Cain was very angry, and his countenance fell. The Lord said to Cain, "Why are you angry, and why has your countenance fallen? If you do well, will you not be accepted? And if you do not do well, sin is couching at the door; its desire is for you, but you must master it."

Cain said to Abel his brother, "Let us go out to the field." And when they were in the field, Cain rose up against his brother Abel, and killed him. Then the Lord said to Cain, "Where is Abel your brother?" He said, "I do not know; am I my brother's keeper?" And the Lord said, "What have you done? The voice of your brother's blood is crying to me from

16

the ground. And now you are cursed from the ground, which has opened its mouth to receive your brother's blood from your hand. When you till the ground, it shall no longer yield to you its strength; you shall be a fugitive and a wanderer on the earth."

Genesis 4:1–12

We all have a little of Cain in us. The story is not told so that we can simply say: People are just mean! That is a very stupid, very blind reaction to the story. If we want to be honest about this story, then we would have to come to the conclusion: That's something even I could have done! That's something I have wanted to do: to really do someone in! Jesus made this very clear in his Sermon on the Mount:

You have heard that it was said to the men of old, "You shall not kill; and whoever kills shall be liable to judgment." But I say to you that every one who is angry with his brother shall be liable to judgment; whoever insults his brother shall be liable to the council, and whoever says "You fool!" shall be liable to the hell of fire.

Matthew 5:21–22

We all have something in us of Cain, the murderer of his brother. It is something we can change and overcome when we recognize it and detect it. That is why religion speaks about sin and guilt. In the churches there is often too much talk about sin and guilt, but no one tells us how we can be free of it. In the churches the issue of sin often gets distorted: nothing is said about the great sins—killing, maiming, starving—rather everything revolves around sinning over sex. In the Cain story, where the word "sin" first appears in the Bible, nothing is said about sex. God's interest is in how we can live *with one another* and how we can be of help to one another in our lives. Each person is to be the guardian and keeper of the other. The great sin which separates us from God and brings us to hate ourselves, as Cain did, is to sin *against* other people: to envy them, to hate them, to shove them out of our way, to have no interest in seeing them at all.

At the beginning of the Bible God asks every person the two most important questions. The first is: "Where are you?" (Genesis 3:9). The second is: "Where is Abel your brother?" (Genesis 4:9). It is we who must live with these questions and give an answer to them. Should we answer with Cain and say: I don't know where my brother and my sister are—they make no difference to me. Whether

17

they are in a refugee camp or live as an old woman around the corner, what does it have to do with me—am I my brother's keeper?

Or are we able to find a better answer to these questions?

A friend of ours who used to be a prison chaplain told us a story. In a New York prison there was a young black man who had killed his mother. Our friend spoke with him once about how understandable it can be that such a thing could have happened, considering the poverty-stricken neighborhood in which they lived, the close living conditions, the broken families, with no hope for employment and wages, with alcoholic and drug-dependent people who saw no meaning in their lives.

While our friend continued to count off the possible social influences which can lead to such a crime, the black man suddenly shouted at him:

"Why don't you cut that nonsense! I've killed my mother! That's not something you can just talk away for me. The guilt belongs to me; it is mine; it does not belong to the conditions we lived in!"

This young man understood that guilt is a part of human worth.

If someone wants to talk me out of my guilt, then he is not taking me very seriously. Instead he is trying to trick me out of being what I really am. In that case he is taking away from me something which belongs to my very life. We might also say: he's talking God out of my life and instead is giving me a little environmental psychology. It belongs to the greatness of the human being, that he is capable of guilt. Only as such is he able to turn away from guilt—and toward life.

Grace: The Best Thing in Life Really Is Free

I had an old aunt who really wasn't liked by anyone in our family. She did everything she could to ingratiate herself to us. She never forgot a birthday. If anyone got sick, she jumped right in to help. In the hard years after the war one of us children had to eat at her house every Sunday. Even though the food was better at her house than at ours, for us these Sundays were the pits. We would have rather stayed home. But our hunger was bigger than our pride. As far as our family was concerned, our aunt was both indispensable and yet at the same time unbearable. Of course, she always expected certain things in return for those Sunday meals and for all the other things she did for the family. For her birthday we had to come up with especially good presents for her. We had to pay her regular visits. Whenever the family had to make an important decision, she claimed the right to have her say in the discussion. So there we were—obligated to see her as our most beloved and indispensable relative. It wasn't that she was mean, not at all. It was just that she always knew exactly what and how much she had done for the rest of us. And she was absolutely convinced that everyone had to love her for it. She believed that she deserved our love and affection. It's a sad story. The highest thing that she could deserve was our meager gratitude.

A short time ago in the course of its programs for economic belt tightening the German government attempted to limit its subsidies for homes for the aged, subsidies which are already slim enough. The basic idea behind this is the same one that my old aunt had: the one who achieves something gets something. The one who doesn't achieve anything or can't produce anything doesn't get anything. This is a merciless proposition. It leads to the conclusion that the

19

worth of those human beings who accomplish the least, or who no longer "deliver," is strongly diminished. Examples of this can be found in prisons, homes for the aged, and mental institutions. In all such places human society offers their inhabitants not what they need but what they deserve. And since they produce so little, they deserve little more than bare subsistence.

There are many stories in the Bible that speak out against such notions of reward for achievement. One of the most vivid is the following:

> And he said, "There was a man who had two sons; and the younger of them said to his father, 'Father, give me the share of property that falls to me.' And he divided his living between them. Not many days later, the younger son gathered all he had and took his journey into a far country, and there he squandered his property in loose living. And when he had spent everything, a great famine arose in that country, and he began to be in want. So he went and joined himself to one of the citizens of that country, who sent him into his fields to feed swine. And he would gladly have fed on the pods that the swine ate; and no one gave him anything. But when he came to himself he said, 'How many of my father's hired servants have bread enough and to spare, but I perish here with hunger! I will arise and go to my father, and I will say to him, "Father, I have sinned against heaven and before you; I am no longer worthy to be called your son; treat me as one of your hired servants."' And he arose and came to his father. But while he was yet at a distance, his father saw him and had compassion, and ran and embraced him and kissed him. And the son said to him, 'Father, I have sinned against heaven and before you; I am no longer worthy to be called your son.' But the father said to his servants, 'Bring quickly the best robe, and put it on him; and put a ring on his hand, and shoes on his feet; and bring the fatted calf and kill it, and let us eat and make merry; for this my son was dead, and is alive again; he was lost, and is found.' And they began to make merry."
>
> Luke 15:11–24

The younger son leaves his father and his family in the lurch. The family's hard-earned wealth he squanders and blows away over night. He leads a thoughtless and inconsiderate life. And suddenly he has nothing left. He looks for but can't even get pig fodder to eat. Now in those days pigs were considered unclean and disgusting, so eating their fodder had to be the absolutely last thing in the world that a human being could possibly stomach. But then the playboy son remembered his father. He went back home to his father, even though he knew that he was entitled to nothing any more, not even to be called his father's son.

He can make no claims any longer, for there is nothing to his credit. Were we to write an ending to this story, we could think of a few different ones. A harsher but perhaps not unfamiliar conclusion is that the father turns the son away by saying: You made your own decision for your life. Now live with it and fend for yourself.

Another conclusion might be that the father takes this son in, gives him something to eat, but then treats him like the family failure, embarrassed to be seen with him in public and never speaking openly about him.

But this story continues differently: the father behaves almost ridiculously. He sees the son coming at a distance and runs on his aging legs to meet him. Just as the son is ready to begin his apology, which he had been practicing on the way, the father kisses him. The son is not hidden from public view either. Everyone gets to participate in his homecoming. The father does not say: See, I told you so! Instead he throws a party. Then he really overdoes it: he has the best clothes brought to his son, the fatted calf is slaughtered and prepared for the celebration, and he even gives his son an expensive ring—in this situation all this appears to us to be a bit excessive.

The Christian tradition has a word for the way this father acted toward his lost son. That word is *grace*.

Perhaps we are unable to appreciate this word, since it has been so often misused. Sometimes the word is used to indicate the favor shown by a person of higher standing toward one of lower standing, or of a strong person toward a weak person, a rich person toward a poor person, a worthy toward an unworthy. When the word "grace" is used in this way it then offends the recipient of grace by emphasizing his unworthiness and the superiority of the grace giver. The word "grace" does not mean the exaltedness of the one over the other. Grace means that we cannot buy the things that give richness and value to our life—neither can we earn them nor achieve them by our own efforts. Friendship, love, the affection of others, forgiveness—

such things are not earned, nor do they have a price. We receive them without cost; they are given to us. We must wait for them and do not need to pay for them.

"I don't want anything to be *given* to me" is something often said by self-sufficient people. But we can't be satisfied with only what we have earned. That would offer far too little in life. The older we get and the more we notice how paltry our achievements really are, it is all the more important that we are able to receive more than what we only have a right to claim.

I once asked an older man what he understood by the term "grace." He answered by telling a little story: "I was in Russia first as a soldier and then afterward as a prisoner. I worked with a farmer whose two sons had been killed by the Germans. The farmer allowed me to sleep at night along with the family next to the warm Russian stove. They put up with the fact that every now and then during the night I touched them. For me that was grace."

The Russian family whose sons had been murdered did not berate this prisoner for what he was, a German and a member of a murderous army. They shared with him what they had: their warmth and their humanity.

Miracle: The Lame Walk

In our everyday parlance we have a number of proverbs and sayings that express the hopelessness with which people view themselves and their lives:

The apple doesn't fall too far from the tree.

What you don't learn as a child you won't learn as an adult.

Little people can't change anything.

Don't trust anyone over thirty.

All these statements have one thing in common: they see the future only as a continuation of the past. Something new, something different, a change in the human being is out of the question. The human being is a victim of his or her past and future, and that's the way it will always be. *The apple doesn't fall too far from the tree*—that means that a person's origin, his or her father and mother, the present circumstances of his or her life will determine the way it will always be for that person. Anyone who hopes for a real change, a real difference in life, is a fool.

Little people can't change anything. There are people who are known as "little people," people who have little clout regarding their own living conditions, and it is often said that nothing will ever change for them. Poor people in particular have such ideas about themselves. Poverty enslaves people not only with regard to their external living conditions, namely that they are unemployed, do not have enough food to eat, and don't have a decent roof over their heads. But poverty also affects people's souls. For they lose faith that they can change anything and that they themselves can do anything about their own situation. Because they have given up hope, they lose the ability to project ahead and to compete with others. They wait around submissively, and they hope that if they're submissive enough they won't be completely destroyed by the worst of life's catastrophes. If only they keep hoping—it's kind of like playing the lottery. They hope that maybe one day Lady Luck will smile on them, that their number will come up, even if the prospects are one in a million. It is noteworthy that playing the lottery has spread most widely among those who have the least to put into it. In Latin America the streets are full of people selling lottery tickets. What little the poor do have is placed on the big number and not on their own strengths and abilities. They don't think much of those things, because the little guy can't change anything anyway.

What makes the Bible such a valuable resource for us is that it is full of stories about change. It is full of miracle stories. Here is one of them:

> And getting into a boat he crossed over and came to his own city. And behold, they brought to him a paralytic, lying on his bed; and when Jesus saw their faith he said to the paralytic, "Take heart, my son; your sins are forgiven." And behold, some of the scribes said to themselves, "This man is blaspheming." But Jesus, knowing their thoughts, said, "Why do you think evil in your hearts? For which is easier, to say, 'Your sins are forgiven,' or to say, 'Rise and walk'? But that you may know that the Son of man has authority on earth to forgive sins"—he then said to the paralytic—"Rise, take up your bed and go home." And he rose and went home. When the crowds saw it, they were afraid, and they glorified God, who had given such authority to men.
>
> Matthew 9:1–8

A paralyzed person is someone who has to watch life virtually pass him by. He can shape his life very little, and he can't take hold of it and do with it what he pleases. As far as his destiny is concerned, he is helpless as a child. Sometimes we have nightmares in which we face some great danger—a fire threatening to consume us or someone following us—and we seem to be paralyzed. We see the way out of the danger, but we can't move our hands and feet. We can't even use our voices to call for help.

Such a paralyzed person was brought to Jesus. Now Jesus does not just put him on his feet and send him on his way. Before his legs and arms are healed there is something else to do: his sins must be forgiven. That is, the invalid must be rid of his indifference toward his own future and be rid of his despair and hopelessness. When that has happened and when the invalid has turned to a new confidence for living, then the healing of his body is something that is not just externally achieved, as if Jesus is the healer and he alone the healed. Then the healing is not just a stroke of luck happening *to* him. The change, the miracle, is brought about by both healer and healed, by Jesus and the invalid, who now views his fate as no longer permanent and unalterable. Now he knows that the miracle is not one great big exception like the winning number in the lottery. Now he knows that miracle is meant for everyone and should be claimed by all who need it.

The miracle stories in the New Testament talk about human lives being changed, even though the prospects for change at first seemed hopeless. The proverbs which we mentioned earlier can now be translated into the language of the New Testament:

The fate of the apple is not determined by the lazy branch from which it has fallen.

The adult may learn what the child has missed.

The little people can get together and become strong and teach the powerful to respect them.

Changing and getting a new grasp on life can be done by older people too.

The New Testament is a rather unashamedly impudent book. Nothing stays the way it is: the lame do not remain lame, lepers do not remain unclean, the poor will have enough for their lives, the mighty do not stay mighty, and tyrants are overthrown. Life is possible for everyone, even when everything seems otherwise.

The miracle stories are stories of revolt against resignation and against the destruction of life. They are stories that teach people not to call it quits, not to satisfy themselves with mediocre and lazy lives. You have a right to life in all its wholeness.

Are these miracles unique with Jesus, or can they happen today? Let us tell you a modern story of miraculous change, the story of a school in Barbiana, Italy.

In the 1960s an Italian priest got together with some young people between the ages of eleven and eighteen who had been expelled from the public schools because they had failed their exams. Both the children and their parents were not particularly surprised that they had been expelled from school.

"Our parents are just farmers," they said. "And farmers don't know much about studying and books."

That is the way they dealt with their own guilt for failing. They had resigned themselves into thinking, That's life. They had not believed that they could possibly be capable of learning and of changing their lives for the better, just like the paralyzed man who saw himself without a future.

Then along came this pastor who got them together in two rooms in his parish house. He not only taught them the subjects that were required in the public school but saw to it that each student immediately became a tutor in his or her own school. The ones who were a little better than the others in math shared their knowledge with those who had trouble in that subject. Others were a bit better in Italian or in spelling, so they didn't keep their abilities to themselves but became the tutors of those who had trouble in language study. The main thing about this school was not that the students gained in knowledge, but that they were able to view themselves in a different light. No longer did they say: I'm a poor farmer's kid, and I don't understand anything about all this. That's the way it is with farmers! They discovered that they could do something and that their abilities could be used by the community in which they lived. As they experienced the fact that they were important to others and that they could learn like everyone else, they then wanted to learn. And they wanted to learn almost incessantly, without interruption. They became excited by this new experience: We can learn, we are not ignorant. We were not the ones who failed; the public school failed in dealing with us.

This was similar to the forgiveness of sins in the story of the paralyzed man. They quit despairing about themselves. They believed something was possible for them. The students in the Barbiana school learned not only physical laws and spelling. They learned where the despair of farmers and where the timidity of their children come from. They learned that there were many unemployed people in Italy. They learned where it is that black people are oppressed and in which countries people are tortured. That was a practical and relevant geography lesson.

These farm children, who in the public schools could hardly speak a connected sentence because of embarrassment, wrote a book in the form of a letter to a teacher, in which they exposed the errors of the public schools and described their own school. This book was not written by professors of pedagogy, but by farm children, who at the age of eleven or twelve years now easily breezed through their exams. That is the miracle: the dumb learn to speak, the disadvantaged no longer allow themselves to be written off as ignorant, the weak recognize their strengths.

Creation: Behold, It Was All Very Good

Often I have to think of the dead fish. I still vividly remember the dead fish. I still have vivid memories of the day a friend of mine and I were walking along the Rhine when suddenly she stopped and said: "Look, over there!" She had become very pale. Then I saw it too: dead fish, a whole procession of them floating belly up downstream.

I think of fish as especially lively creatures, quick and full of movement. Beautiful, shiny, and silvery, they are not caught easily, and they find their own ways through the expansive waters.

Why were these fish dead? We made it a point to learn more about the chemical waste dumped by industries into our rivers. Entire animal species have become extinct. Birds don't come back any more because their nesting places have been destroyed. Even plants and trees no longer have enough air to breathe, or enough water, or are simply removed. Entire forests, which serve as recreational areas for people who live in the big cities, have been cut down and cleared, in order to create still more business for the airlines or even to accommodate military airplanes equipped with bombs. Slowly but surely we are ruining the earth we live on, without consideration for those who will live on it after us.

The Bible speaks out against this, too. This is not the way things were meant to be. Life on earth does not come from itself, nor is it simply there, like a pile of rocks lying on a mountainside. The Bible tells us that God has created everything. That is not meant to contradict natural science, as if we could chart the origin of species from the Bible, or as if to say that the religious person knows more about nature than the scientist. The issue here is not knowledge as such, but behavior. How are we to behave toward the earth we live on?

Creation: Behold, It Was All Very Good

When we hear a story like God creating all things, we should start wondering what question is being answered by such a story. I think that people (children, for example) who want to know something about themselves and our earth ask: Where does everything come from? And why is all this here?

Science tries to explain the first question, but it is basically oblivious to the second. It is self-evident that everything is here to fulfill our needs and to be used according to our desires (science says). Nature is *material* which people can utilize. We are the masters and nature belongs to us. We possess it like property holders. But the Bible says: "The earth is the Lord's and the fulness thereof" (Psalm 24:1).

Many farm people have organized for action when the land around them begins to be subdivided, and the open fields are privately bought and sold as marketable property. They have constantly taken a position on the basis of the ancient decree, "The earth is the Lord's." Even today in the liberation movements of Latin America this statement plays an important role: the land belongs neither to the big land developers nor to the engineers who want it for their oil or raw materials and who, for example, drive out the native tribes dwelling in the Brazilian forest or exterminate them with poison gas. The Eskimos, the Hopi Indians, the original native Australians have an entirely different relationship with the earth. They say that the earth knows nothing about the words "mine" and "yours."

A few years ago in Bavaria, where the land around most of the lakes is privately owned, there was a dispute over the issue of whether vacationers had access to the shores of the lakes. People still felt that a lake belongs to everyone, even to those who want to go swimming or fishing, and that it can't be fenced off by private landowners. The land belongs to God—that means that it is not a marketable item which can be picked up for the best possible price like a pair of shoes or an automobile. We can't reproduce the earth. It doesn't come from a factory; it comes from God. If the earth belongs to God then it belongs at the same time to everyone else. A property owner can possess certain items, but what right does he have to think that he can own the earth (as his own possession)? Maybe next he will claim the air over his piece of earth and perhaps also the water that runs through it! That owner did not create the earth.

To believe in creation means two things. First of all, it means that the earth is not to be recklessly dominated, subjugated, subdued, and exploited. Second, creation means that the earth is not to be parceled out among "owners" and "possessors," as if everything—the desert, the ocean, the animals, the plants—has to belong to somebody! We can only manage what already belongs to God; we are trustees of the creation. When we speak of creation we mean that everything comes from God and that everything continues to belong to him and not some things to a few. In the Bible there is a certain communism of the earth.

That we are trustees of the creation is something I first understood when I had children and became a mother. Children are borne by us parents, but they are created by God. God loans them to us for fifteen or twenty years. They are never our possession, because they belong to God. No person can possess another. I am not only my parents' son or daughter but a creature of God.

The Bible speaks out against this notion of possession. It speaks in a different way about plants and animals, energy and raw materials.

> The sea, so great and wide, teeming with a multitude innumerable, so many small creatures, so many large. There go the ships on their way, there is the gigantic leviathan, whom you made to play with. All eyes wait upon you, on food which you give at the proper time. You open your hand and they are filled, you take away their breath, and they die.
>
> Psalm 104:25–29 (Soelle)

God created leviathan, the gigantic water monster—translators used to think this referred to the whale—for the purpose of playing with it. It is not there simply to be commercially profitable, simply to produce something. All created life, even animals and plants, has reason in itself for being. It doesn't have to yield some kind of profit for human beings. It doesn't belong to those who want to exploit it. It belongs to God, to life itself. When we use the word "nature" for all that exists, we shall think only of what we can use, what we can explore, and what we can control. But when we use the word "creation" for all that exists, we shall begin to have that "respect for life" of which the great doctor Albert Schweitzer spoke.

Many religions know more about creation than we white people do in the Western world. Native Americans fought against immigrant Europeans because they had a different relationship with nature, with wild plants and animals, with sun and earth, than that of the white invaders.

The native American chief Seattle of the Squawmish and Duwamish tribes in the area of Washington state wrote a famous letter in 1855 to the President of the United States, the great chief in Washington, D.C., who wanted to buy more land from the Indians:

> We know that the white man does not understand our ways. To him, one piece of land is like any other, for he is a stranger who comes in the night and takes from the earth whatever he always needs. The earth is not his brother, but his enemy, and when he has conquered it, he moves on. He leaves the graves of his fathers behind—and cares about them no more. He steals the earth from his children—and cares about it no more. He treats his mother, the earth, and his brother, the sky, like things he can purchase and plunder, as if they were for sale like sheep or shiny pearls. His hunger will devour the earth and leave nothing behind but a desert.

Whoever believes in God will not deal with nature like the people, for example, who want to build the runway west of the Frankfurt airport. This issue is not just about what is practical, or how we can get from one place to another faster. This issue has to do with how we are to treat the creation: with respect and full consideration for it, keeping in mind those human beings who will live after us, and who do not want to live in a world of concrete buildings with polluted water and dead forests around them.

> The air is precious for the red man—for all things share the same breath—the animal, the tree, the human being—they all share the same breath. The white man seems not to notice the air he breathes; like a person who has been dead for several days, he is oblivious to the stench. What is the human being without the animals? Were there no animals, the human being would die of loneliness of spirit. Whatever happens to animals will soon happen to human beings. All things are bound together with each other. What happens to the earth, happens to the sons of the earth. For this we know: the earth does not belong to the human being—the human being belongs to the earth. For he did not create the web of life; he is only a fiber within it. What you do to the web, you do also to yourself.

When we say that God is on the side of the small, the weak, the one who needs our protection, then he also is on the side of creation. The big game hunter who goes after animals with floodlights, encircling them and gunning them down, is not particularly masculine or courageous or heroic, even if he thinks he is. He cares nothing about the course of life which dwells in the animals, in the plants, as well as in us ourselves: the being born, the maturing, the giving birth, and the dying. He sees only things, not life. Whoever enslaves nature and despoils it will not behave any better than a slave owner, even toward other human beings.

A story that is not in the Bible but comes from early Christianity deals with our relationship to the animals.

> Jesus went with his disciples outside the city. They came to a road going up a steep hill and met a man with his beast of burden. The animal had fallen down because the man had overloaded it. He kept hitting it until it began to bleed.
>
> Jesus went over to him and said, "Sir, why are you hitting that animal? Don't you see that it is too weak for the load you've put on him? Don't you know that it is suffering?"
>
> The man answered, "What should you care about it? I can beat it as much as I want to. I've paid good money for it and it's my property. Ask the people standing around you if that isn't so. They know who I am."
>
> Some of the disciples said, "The man is right. We saw it when he bought the animal."
>
> But Jesus went on to say to them, "Don't you see that it is bleeding? And don't you hear how it is yelling and screaming?"
>
> They answered, "No, Lord, we don't hear it yelling and screaming."
>
> Then Jesus said, "That's bad for you, that you don't hear how it is yelling and screaming for mercy to God who created it! And doubly bad for you, sir, that you don't hear who this animal is yelling and screaming about in his pain."
>
> And Jesus touched the animal. It stood up and his wounds were closed/healed. But to the man Jesus went on to say: "You can lead it on now. But in the future do not beat it again, so that you will receive mercy yourself."

We recently read a good story about ten children in Göglingen who prevented the destruction of their chestnut tree when their street was to be widened. Together they wrote to the city council:

Creation: Behold, It Was All Very Good

"The chestnut tree is our friend. When it rains it is our roof, and when it is hot it gives us shade." The city council respected the children and followed what they said. It is really good that children find friendship not only with human beings or with animals but also with a tree. We can thereby learn to see again the secret of creation: the chestnut tree is our friend.

Freedom: No One Is Powerless

I remember something that happened forty years ago when I was in school, and it still makes me angry. Someone had stolen some money from our class treasury, and our teacher tried to find out who the guilty person was, but without success. At the time there was a rather quiet boy in our class. His father had been in prison for quite a while. There were too many children in his family, and the family was seen as "antisocial." That's what they often used to call people in Germany back then who, because of their poverty and their many children, had a hard time in life. The teacher called this boy to the front of the class, slapped him several times across the face, and said to him: "You must have been the one. And if it wasn't you then let this swatting be a lesson to you anyway."

The boy went silently back to his desk, and the rest of us didn't say a word. We chickened out and were glad we weren't the one who got it. Generally, this teacher wasn't particularly mean. In his anger he had simply made use of his power: the power to slap another person, one who was weaker than he, the power to violate the self-respect of this boy and to declare him a thief. Even the rest of us were injured by his power and domineering authority. He had brought us to the point of cowardice by our remaining silent about this injustice, and thereby betraying our solidarity with our classmate.

In the Bible we find a number of stories that speak out against the use of power by one person over another. One of them is in one of the very earliest books of the Old Testament, the Book of Judges:

A man by the name of Abimelech presented himself to the people as their ruler. The people gave him silver from the temple treasury. With it he bought a hired soldier with whose help he killed all his opponents. After these murders the people by no means stopped wanting him as their ruler. They even crowned him their king. Despotism and brute force not only seem to offend people, but they also make an impression on them. Maybe back then people thought as they do now: Finally we have someone who does something! At last we have someone with a strong hand!

At that time someone resisted such a notion and circulated the following satirical fable:

> The trees once went forth to anoint a king over them; and they said to the olive tree, "Reign over us." But the olive tree said to them, "Shall I leave my fatness, by which gods and men are honored, and go to sway over the trees?" And the trees said to the fig tree, "Come you, and reign over us." But the fig tree said to them, "Shall I leave my sweetness and my good fruit, and go to sway over the trees?" And the trees said to the vine, "Come you, and reign over us." But the vine said to them, "Shall I leave my wine which cheers gods and men, and go to sway over the trees?" Then all the trees said to the bramble, "Come you and reign over us." And the bramble said to the trees, "If in good faith you are anointing me king over you, then come and take refuge in my shade; but if not, let fire come out of the bramble and devour the cedars of Lebanon."
>
> Judges 9:8–15

In times of tyranny and dictatorial oppression one's manner of speaking must be altered in order that the ruler's informers cannot immediately understand what is being said. It is a sort of code language, rich in symbolic speech and secret jargon.

The satire in Judges 9 is an example of such expression and at first hearing is not understandable. The trees who want a king are those people who cannot bear being free and having no one to rule over them. They surrender their freedom because they think so little of themselves and of others. They believe that they are not strong, responsible, and solvent enough to make their own decisions. So these people go out and look for a king. They come to three big and beautiful *trees* bearing vital fruits: an olive tree, a fig tree, and a grapevine. These trees—symbolic pictures of independent, self-sufficient human beings who are not willing to sell their self-dignity—refuse the offer. They say that ruling over others not only disgraces those others but would also destroy those who rule. We would be abandoning our fatness, our sweetness, and our wine.

Whoever rules over another cripples himself and becomes unfruitful, they say. Since none of the splendid and fruit-laden trees would become king, the trees then asked the thornbush. The bramble had no figs, no olives, no grapes. It had only its sharp thorns and its shadeless branches. Of course this thornbush, which could bring nothing but injury, gladly accepted the kingship. And with malicious mockery, the one who was incapable of providing shade offered his branches as a refuge for others.

The Christian churches have so seldom adhered to the stories in their own sacred writings which laugh at power and lordship and demand their abolition. They have adulated powerful tyrants. They have lauded the power of political leaders as God-given, and they have blessed the weapons of the powerful which are used to torture and kill the poor. They have offered prayers for king and emperor. On the belt buckles of the German army were the words "God with us." But the church could never disavow these stories, since they are in their Bible. And there always were Christian groups who *emphasized* them, who appealed to them, and who tried to live by them. Those who have such stories about resistance against political power in the books they treasure cannot be completely neutral and undisturbed about being linked up with political powers that be. Their devotion to power and to the powerful will destroy them. These disturbing words are an advantage that Christians have.

> But you are not to be called rabbi, for you have one teacher, and you are all brethren. And call no man your father on earth, for you have one Father, who is in heaven. Neither be called masters, for you have one master, the Christ. He who is greatest among you shall be your servant; whoever exalts himself will be humbled, and whoever humbles himself will be exalted.
>
> Matthew 23:8–12

There is a story about Francis of Assisi who lived at the end of the twelfth and beginning of the thirteenth centuries. He was extremely suspicious of every ecclesiastical and secular power, and he taught this suspicion to those with whom he came into contact. Francis gathered companions around him who called themselves brothers, and none of them was to be ruled by any of the others.

One day a young brother came to Francis and asked whether he could have as his own possession a book of the psalm tunes sung by the brothers in the worship services. Francis hesitated, and the brother asked him again. Francis finally replied: "If you get this book, then you will want still other and thicker books for yourself alone. And when you get all these books you will want to sit at the lecture desk and say to your brother, 'Brother, come here and bring me my book!'"

This story says to us: the one who has property gains power over other people. He can then say: "Brother, come here and bring me my book." He can command his brother as if he were a thing. As far as he is concerned, the brother is as good as dead, alive only to carry his books. His brother is there only to take orders and to carry them out.

Francis fought against the powerful who oppressed others. He himself lived a kind of freedom.

A student once told us about her grandmother. The woman was a Quaker and belonged to a small church that had no pastors and bishops and lived according to Christian principles. One day the student's grandmother had to go to court, where the judge asked her to rise. "Your honor," she said, "I rise before God, because all honor belongs to him. But before a human being I will not rise." For that she received three days in prison.

When I heard this I thought: That's the kind of grandmother I would like to have.

Prayer: Learning What We Really Want

We had gone to a funeral. A colleague and friend of ours had died suddenly. He was not yet very old. The day before he died we had eaten together and had planned the work we had to do together. He was a good teacher, respected among the students. He stood for what he said. This friend was an intelligent atheist, as was his wife. Both had quit the church. Now we were attending his funeral. We were sitting in the funeral home, with the casket in front of us. We waited silently for about ten minutes. Then the pallbearers took the casket to the hearse, and we went out to the graveside. The casket was lowered, and as the last of the procession arrived the casket was already in the grave. We stood there for another few minutes. Then we went home.

The hopeless silence of this funeral is a terrible memory for us. Everything was crying out inside us: Why did this friend have to die so early in life? What is the meaning of such a death? We were all full of anger and grief, but everyone kept their grief to themselves. It did not come out. It found no expression, no gesture, no hymn song, no curse. We remained speechless. The next day we had a meeting. The chairperson of the meeting referred once again to the death of our colleague and said: "We don't want to make a great speech now. But I will ask you to rise and offer some silent thoughts about the deceased!"

Death is supposed to have no discussion, no expression anymore. The paltry vestiges of expression were limited to rising for a moment, standing there somewhat embarrassed, not knowing what to do with your hands. Everyone was relieved when the chairperson got on with the order of the day.

Prayer: Learning What We Really Want

But can there be any "order of the day" when someone dies? When crucial events happen in our lives, can we simply give up crying, praising, thanking, cursing, screaming, accusing, extolling, celebrating? What would happen to us if our lives were without sound and song? Wouldn't life wither away if we had no language to use for the things which occur?

Finding expression for our desires as well as our hurts is called praying. Prayer plays a big role in Christian tradition. The Bible depicts several situations in which people have prayed in times of misfortune, out of anger, or in times of good fortune. The Bible contains an entire prayer book, namely the Book of Psalms in the Old Testament. Psalm 13 goes like this:

> How long, O Lord, are you always going to forget about me?
> How long are you going to hide your face from me?
> How long must I have pain in my soul, and sorrow in my heart day and
>   night?
> How long is my enemy going to be exalted over me?
> Consider all this and answer me, O Lord my God; light up my eyes, lest I
>   sleep the sleep of death;
> lest my enemy boast, "I have won over him"; lest my foes rejoice
>   because I am shaken.
> But I have trusted in your favor; my heart will rejoice in your help.
> I will sing to the Lord, because he has dealt well with me.
>
> Psalm 13 (Soelle)

We no longer know exactly what misfortune had occurred to the person who originally prayed these words. We do not know who his enemies were against whom he speaks before God. But we like the way this person prayed. First of all, he does something very important: he spells out the issue right away. He doesn't say, Well, that's the way it goes! He identifies the misfortune he has experienced. He does not find his affliction simply acceptable. He directs a few questions to God, almost threateningly: How long are you going to forget me? How long are you going to keep looking away while my enemies persecute me? How long should I allow myself to be ruined? How long should injustice triumph over the poor? The one who raises questions is not resigned to the way things are. Whoever asks questions like this is ready for revolution; he has already taken the first step toward resistance against the injustice that has been done to him and to others. The one who can identify his affliction is the one who can demand reversal.

Look at me, he says to God. I am not going to stay in this death-bound existence. That would not be the weak-hearted language of someone who accepts everything as it comes and who offers up his head for everything. He demands of God what God has promised. I am trusting in you! he says.

To pray means to want something and to want it very much. If you read Psalm 13 slowly you will notice that there is a change in the one who is praying. He moves from lament to petition, from complaint to request, and then on to something that we can call confidence. He becomes calmer, quieter.

When we ask if prayers are ever heard we should take a psalm like this one and try to understand what happens to the one who prays. God is not a machine that we can insert a coin into and then expect to get whatever we want. But prayer changes the one who prays. To really want justice, or victory over injustice, or success and well-being, or a life worth living—to desire these things is not automatic. One must learn to want them. And we learn to want them when we can bring that desire out into expression. The affliction of the poor consists not only in the fact that they have no food or water or clothes. It consists also in the fact that they have lost all inner desire for themselves and that they can hardly envision that life might be otherwise.

To pray is to revolt. The one who prays is not saying, That's the way it is and that's that! The one who prays is saying, That's the way it is, but it should not be that way! And these are the things that must be changed!

Praying is intensive preparation for real life. The well-known leader of farm workers Cesar Chavez, a Catholic, has been fighting for years to ensure that poor Mexican immigrants are not completely without their rights in relation to the big landowners. He has been fighting for contracts and a minimum wage for their work, and so that they are not shot by the landowners when they join forces to achieve their demands. He organizes strikes wherever the exploitation is greatest. He often organizes boycotts against the big landowners who act particularly unjustly. That is, he sees to it that they are unable to sell their lettuce and grapes. For each one of these actions he carefully prepares himself by means of prayer vigils and long periods of fasting. Once before a large and dangerous strike he prayed and fasted for twenty-four days. Each time he prepares himself like this, his opponents say: Watch out, Cesar Chavez is planning something—he's praying!

For this man praying doesn't mean shoving the responsibility off onto God for those things for which we ourselves are responsible. For him prayer means to make God our ally against the abuses and acts of destruction that are directed against the poor, just as it occurs in the psalm we have just read. Why is it so hard for us to pray? Why are we ashamed of our prayers? Why are we laughed at when others find out that we pray? There are many reasons for this. More than anything, it is because prayer is so frequently misused. Certainly it happens that a person in prayer is doing nothing more than muttering in a condition of weakness and hopelessness. But perhaps it also has to do with the fact that our desires and our demands in life are too small. Whoever really wants something cries it out and speaks it; he or she is so obsessed with desires and can't keep them enclosed quietly in the heart. Silent wishes are soon wished no more.

Friends of ours work in a part of the city of Hamburg where foreigners live. More and more they see the injustices that are being done to these people. They see how they are despised, how their schools are inadequate for them, and how bad their housing is. Every Saturday in the marketplace our friends make what they call a public outcry. They pass out information about the conditions in which these foreigners must live. They list their accusations and publish their demands. Prayer is that kind of open outcry before a great witness: before God, who has promised to enter into our lives.

We can learn to pray when we say to God what it is that we really want right now. It can be big, it can be small. It can be about the health of a relative or about a basketball game. We can neither deceive God nor impose something on him. We can only slowly forget God, and that would be terrible since then we would slowly be forgetting ourselves as well.

We have found a good example of prayer, written by an unknown man in Brazil.

Not Just Yes and Amen

An Open Letter to Jesus of Nazareth*

Forgive me for writing to you.
Certainly there isn't much about me that you should care about.
I'm a rather insignificant case: Segundo Lopez Sanchez.
Carpenter by profession, married with five children.
I work for a construction firm and take on odd jobs as they come along.
I am one of your poor.
I have neither the strength nor the patience to go into that.
Lord, the struggle for survival is great, and the booze is running out.
Lord, it would be better if you would come down and see all this with
    your own eyes.
I am not very educated, but it is said that in your youth you had the
    same profession I have.
I don't know what it meant in those days to make a living by working
    and to be poor.
Today, by contrast, it is a miracle to have anything more than a piece of
    bread and fish, if there's anything to put on the table at all, and to be
    able to share it so that everyone receives a little.
You can discover it yourself:
Come and work as a carpenter along with us,
Try to get along on a day's wages.
You'll be sweating blood like you did in the Garden.
Go out into the streets and start preaching like you once did against the
    Pharisees.
Repeat what you said about the rich and the eye of the needle.
Cast the merchants out of the church, and let's see what happens.
If they don't crucify you like they did then it will be because today one
    word is all they need to say to get you to keep silent.
Is that being too facetious?
Lord, come and help us, so that they don't say:
"Even Christ himself can't solve the problem."
From one worker to another I am asking you and affix my signature:
Your humble follower Segundo Lopez Sanchez.

*From *Sehnsucht nach dem Fest der freien Menschen* (*Longing for the Celebration of the
Free*), ed. A. Reiser and P. G. Schoenborn (Wuppertal, 1982).

Discipleship: What You Really Want to Do with Your Life

What is the meaning of life? Why are we even here? What's everything for? And how do I fit into this whole thing? Does it make a difference at all whether I'm here or not? And to whom? People often ask such questions, and no one has to be crazy to do so. On the contrary: those who keep sweeping them under the rug and never get around to thinking about them are the ones who must be pretty lifeless—and need even larger rugs!

Next to the issues of hunger and thirst and justice there is yet another thing that every human being wants, something that is not at all easy to stamp out: it is the desire to be useful. Everyone has to feel needed. I am genuinely happy when I know that it does make a difference whether I am here or not. When we are young it is no great problem yet, because we know that our parents need us and, for example, get nervous when we don't come home on time. When we get older it is not enough that our parents need us. We need to be needed by others. I still remember when I was thirteen and on spring evenings stood next to a cherry tree in bloom. It was then that I consciously for the first time saw the wide open sky with its stars. I knew for the first time that I was alone. It hurt. The friendship and closeness that I experienced with my parents and my brothers and sisters was no longer enough. In spite of all that, I still felt alone.

The crazy question about life's meaning had caught up with me. Books can offer some help in answering these questions, but people are better than books. To be a Christian is something you learn from other people; Christians are, as Paul once said, "a letter from Christ" (2 Corinthians 3:3), written not with ink but with the Spirit of the living God, not etched on tablets of stone but in the heart.

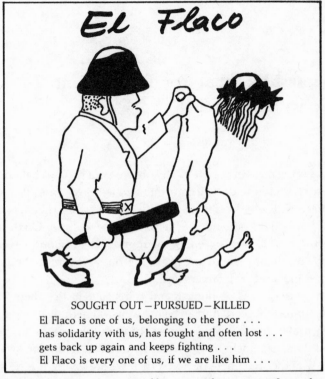

SOUGHT OUT – PURSUED – KILLED

El Flaco is one of us, belonging to the poor . . .
has solidarity with us, has fought and often lost . . .
gets back up again and keeps fighting . . .
El Flaco is every one of us, if we are like him . . .

In Latin America everyone quickly gets a nickname – even Jesus who is depicted on this flyer. Flaco (slim) is no rarity, especially among the poor.

I want to talk about a person who for me has been a letter from Christ. A woman, an American, a Catholic nun. She is one of the four women who in early December 1980 was murdered in El Salvador by the military regime supported by the United States. Why, one asks, is it necessary for the killer commandos of this regime to mistreat, rape, and murder four unarmed women?

In El Salvador a civil war is going on. On the one side stand thirteen rich and powerful families who own virtually the entire country. They have established a military dictatorship which is supported by the North Americans with money, weapons, and so-called advisors, who are military and police specialists. On the other side stand the liberation fighters, who struggle on behalf of the country's poor people for land reform and village schools, and for health care for everyone, apart from wealth and possessions. Ita Ford and her sisters fought not with weapons in their hands. But they stood clearly on the side of the poor, because they knew that Christians have to stand on the side of the people. So they belonged to the thousands of Christians in Latin America who are there for the poor and therefore are pursued, captured, tortured, and murdered.

Ita Ford belonged to the Maryknoll Sisters, a missionary order of women who live not in convents but in the slums together with the poor for whom they are here. They wear no habits but just ordinary clothing. I have seen photographs of Ita Ford, and I thought she looked like a bank teller or perhaps a teacher, a very normal woman of forty years of age, likable, not particularly pretty, trustworthy. This woman has become a letter from Christ for me. Ita Ford was born in 1940 in Brooklyn. When she was 21, after graduating from college, she joined her order and went in 1971 to Chile, soon after the fall of the short-lived socialist regime of Allende. The following years of economic difficulties and political persecution made an impact on her: there she learned what it means as a Christian to make the problems of the poor one's own problems, to live in a *barrio*, a slum, with very few personal things, interrupted day and night by people who need a place to hide and food and clothing. Reflecting on this Ita wrote in 1977:

> Have I been willed to suffer here with the people, to share the pain of the powerless, the feeling of powerlessness? Can I say to my neighbor: I have no solution for this situation, I have no answers, but I want to go with you and look for them with you. Can I allow myself to be evangelized by this opportunity? Am I able to see my own poverty and accept what I learn from others?

Ita Ford learned the lesson of the poor in Chile. When Archbishop Oscar Romero called for help in San Salvador, she was prepared to go there. When she arrived Romero had just been murdered. The new beginning wasn't easy, and she missed her sisters and friends. It was not easy to gain the confidence and trust of people who, terrorized by the political situation, lived in constant fear. She worked in an emergency program for refugees. "I don't know," she wrote, "whether it is in spite of or because of all the horror, the fear, the confusion and the

Oscar Romero

lawlessness, but I do know that it is right for me to be here. I believe that we who are now in and for El Salvador are here so that the necessary questions can be answered, and so that we in faith will one day be together with the Salvadorans, on a road that is now washed out and full of barriers and detours."

Ita and her sisters felt a responsibility for the needs of the wounded, the homeless, and the hungry. It was clear to them what the political consequences are for feeding the hungry in a country involved in an undeclared civil war. There were rumors that her name was on the lists of several right-wing terrorist organizations. At the end of November 1980 Ita went to a conference in Nicaragua. According to reports from her sisters, those five days must have been a time of deep healing for her. At the beginning of her work in El Salvador she had lost her best friend in an accident. At the concluding worship of the conference she read a text from the last sermon of Oscar Romero, a prediction that became true for her a mere twenty-four hours later.

"Christ invites us not to fear persecution because, believe me, brothers and sisters, whoever decides for the poor must endure the same fate as the poor, and in El Salvador we know what the fate of the poor really means: to disappear, to be tortured, to be imprisoned, and to be found dead."

In mid-January about fifteen hundred people participated in a worship service in front of the White House in Washington. It was a memorial service "For the Four and Ten Thousand" who had been murdered the previous year in El Salvador. Four white caskets were carried to the Capitol building, and there was a large symbolic casket for the many others, for the most part defenseless victims, children, young people, *campesinos*, and women, who were suspected as *subversive* and *terroristic* and were murdered.

There is a hope out of which people like Ita Ford live. The Bible speaks like this about that authentic life which has a meaning:

> For this is the message which you have heard from the beginning, that we should love one another, and not be like Cain who was of the evil one and murdered his brother. And why did he murder him? Because his own deeds were evil and his brother's righteous. Do not wonder, brethren, that the world hates you. We know that we have passed out of

47

death into life, because we love the brethren. He who does not love abides in death. Any one who hates his brother is a murderer, and you know that no murderer has eternal life abiding in him. By this we know love, that he laid down his life for us; and we ought to lay down our lives for the brethren. But if any one has the world's goods and sees his brother in need, yet closes his heart against him, how does God's love abide in him? Little children, let us not love in word or speech but in deed and in truth.

1 John 3:11–18

In August 1980 Ita Ford wrote a birthday letter to her sixteen-year-old niece Jennifer. I would like to convey from this letter, which was given to me by one of the Maryknoll sisters, something of the spirit of people like Ita and Maura and Dorothy and Jean.

Dear Jennifer,

It is possible that this birthday greeting won't get to you, but you know that I'm with you in spirit when you celebrate your Sixteenth! I hope it will be a special day for you. I want to say something to you and I wish I could be there to talk with you, because thoughts and feelings sometimes don't get across in letters. But I'll try anyway. More than anything else I love you and am thinking about you and how well things are going for you. But you know that already, and that is true whether you are an angel or a rascal, a genius or a dunce. A lot depends on you and what you decide to do with your life. Much of what I have to say to you is not just cheery birthday chatter, but very true: yesterday I stood out on the street and saw a sixteen-year-old who had been killed a couple hours before. I know of a number of children even younger who are dead. It is a terrible time in El Salvador for young people right now. So much idealism and involvement is crushed to the ground. The reasons why so many people are killed are pretty complicated, but there are a couple that are rather clear and simple. One is that many people have discovered something worth living, sacrificing, fighting, and even dying for! Whether their lives last sixteen, sixty, or ninety years, their lives have meaning for them. In many respects they have it quite good.

The same thing isn't happening in Brooklyn as it is in El Salvador. But a few things remain true wherever we are and no matter how old we are. What I want to say is this: I hope you get to discover that which gives life a deep meaning for you. Something worth living for, perhaps even something worth dying for, which gives you strength and excites you and enables you to go on.

I can't tell you what that should be. You have to discover it yourself, to

decide for it and love it. I can only encourage you to keep looking for it
and I will support you as you do.

I understand this letter to say: you are responsible for the meaning
which you give to your life. Even if you are sixteen years old you can
give some direction to your life. A Jewish proverb says: "The world
was created in order to give a choice to those who want to make
choices." But many people see themselves no longer in the position to
choose at all between meaningless and meaningful employment;
between so many different meaningless consumer pressures, it's all
the same anyway what one does. Many feel that their lives have been
decided somewhere else, that they function only as programmed
objects. I think that Ita Ford's letter to her sixteen-year-old niece is an
example of having the highest respect for life, for it does not allow
anyone to think so little of themselves. It has something to do with
the pride of being a human being and not a statistical number. We do
not live our lives like puppets on a string. We love the ability to make
choices between various possibilities. It is possible to become a letter
from Christ, written for life, for happiness, and for justice.

Perhaps many of you are thinking right now: But we aren't in El
Salvador. And we can't all be missionaries or social workers. What
are *we* supposed to do with this example of a Christian life? Such a
way of thinking, in my opinion, is a cop-out. As if we didn't want to
read a letter from Christ! Ita Ford doesn't tell her niece to leave Brooklyn, to become a nun, or to go to El Salvador. But she calls her to
another way of life, one different from what we normally or maybe
even unconsciously allow to be made of ours. And that is exactly
what a letter from Christ, which we can all be, is supposed to contain. An invitation to life, to wholeness, to authenticity. Come on, it
says in this letter which we have received and which we can become,
it is fortunate to be alive. To be loved and learn to love, to be dealt
with justly and to stand up for justice, to be at peace and to work for
peace. The kingdom of God is lived here and now—and that is what
is written in a letter from Christ.

If we are honest then we know that we can make choices, that we
have different possibilities, that it makes a difference how we deal

with our time, our money, and our ability. If we live authentically, then we shall live ever more openly for others. The message of the letter, its content, will be inseparable from us. We, who have something to hope for, who learn to believe even when we are tempted to think too little of ourselves, we who are able to love even when we are full of fear—we are the message, we are a letter from Christ, an invitation to life.

Faith: All Things Are Possible

A central area of our lives is the work we do. When we reflect in this book about the worth of the human being, what a remarkable thing of beauty he is, and how he can be his brother's *keeper*, then all this must apply as well during the time when he is at work.

A Bavarian youth representative tells a story about the youth line at Siemens*:

It's been decided that young people who are unemployed, like those who have just finished high school, should be off the streets. But now only girls get jobs working on the youth line because they're cheap labor. It's different from the normal line, where everyone gets one whole machine and not just a couple levers. So what? A couple more levers don't make an education. Why do they do this? Because it's unbelievably profitable. The company gets a grant from the employment agency for the jobs it offers, and the wages for girls are small. They're placed in category 02, that is, they get 650 German marks right now. Every month. That way the management kills the motivation for a teaching position. Because if the ones who are now used to getting paid like that want to go teach, they might get only 200 German marks. That means that you can't get anybody excited about a teaching position after that. So that's it. For management that's good, for youth it's bad. Because they really don't learn a job, a profession, but they just learn to work, assembly-line work at that, and from their first breath to their last they produce for the company. At first slowly, and they get paid less for it, then more. As assembly-line specialists. As it turns out, management gets credit for keeping people off the streets—as assembly-line monkeys, if you will, without profession, knowledge, prospect for the future. And then: whoever's been standing at an assembly line since he

*F. X. Kroetz, *Chiemgauer Geschichten, Bayerische Menschen erzählen* (*Chiemgau Stories as Told by Bavarians*).

was fifteen years old knows nothing else; how *can* he know anything else? Management can do whatever they want with them. Whoever doesn't know any better doesn't want to know better, that's for sure. OK, how else? What real employment is, where you can develop some ideas, where you can somehow enjoy life to the fullest, where you can even gain something that can make you happy—these people never know such things. From the very first the only thing they know is: work, work those levers as fast as you can. Work is to turn off your brain and be glad when the day is done. For these people work is, if you will, the opposite of living. But you have to do it so that you can live.

How would someone in the Bible react to this story? Since the creation of humanity, labor has been a part of human life. Even in Paradise Adam and Eve were gardeners. We are created in the image of God. This does not mean that we are supposed to look like God (and that God looks like an old white male), but that we are able to act like God. That we are able to make a change in our environment; that we are often able to bring joy out of grief; that we are creative. God is the creator, just like workers, the Creator of all the things we need.

This isn't very noticeable in our everyday reality. The young girls who were trained by Siemens to be "assembly-line monkeys" have it relatively good. Many others have absolutely no prospect for any kind of employment or training. The hopes in life for many young people are limited already from the start, the world boarded up and nailed shut. To have no hope means also to have no pride in being human, no joy in being able to learn something and to develop oneself and one's own strengths.

Our ability to be happy has much to do with our ability to work. But we are not thinking here of the kind of work that brings us nothing but money; we are thinking of genuinely fulfilling work. We can't allow ourselves to be talked out of that, for every human being also has a right to come to a realization of himself in his work.

But isn't that completely impossible, unrealistic, utopian? Is it a dream or does it contain some reality? We usually think in terms of what is possible, what is attainable. It's like our lives were running on tracks like a railroad train. The tracks, the signals, the conducting—all that is already there. We can see other trains along the way or we can even see that they travel faster, but the latitude between what is possible and what is impossible is very limited. All that is different with Jesus.

> And when they came to the disciples, they saw a great crowd about them, and scribes arguing with them. And immediately all the crowd, when they saw him, was greatly amazed, and ran up to him and greeted him. And he asked them, "What are you discussing with them?" And one of the crowd answered him, "Teacher, I brought my son to you, for he has a dumb spirit; and wherever it seizes him, it dashes him down; and he foams and grinds his teeth and becomes rigid; and I asked your disciples to cast it out, and they were not able." And he answered them, "O faithless generation, how long am I to be with you? How long am I to bear with you? Bring him to me." And they brought the boy to him; and when the spirit saw him, immediately it convulsed the boy, and he fell on the ground and rolled about, foaming at the mouth. And Jesus asked his father, "How long has he had this?" And he said, "From childhood. And it has often cast him into the fire and into the water, to destroy him; but if you can do anything, have pity on us and help us." And Jesus said to him, "If you can! All things are possible to him who believes." Immediately the father of the child cried out and said, "I believe, help my unbelief!" And when Jesus saw that a crowd came running together, he rebuked the unclean spirit, saying to it, "You dumb and deaf spirit, I command you, come out of him, and never enter him again." And after crying out and convulsing him terribly, it came out, and the boy was like a corpse; so that most of them said, "He is dead." But Jesus took him by the hand and lifted him up, and he arose. And when he had entered the house, his disciples asked him privately, "Why could we not cast it out?" And he said to them, "This kind cannot be driven out by anything but prayer."
>
> Mark 9:14–29

Jesus' friends got into an argument with the scribes over what is *possible*. The friends of Jesus tried to heal the boy who was physically sick and had often tried to commit suicide. But like everyone who has tried to help people who are drug-dependent and depression-prone, they come to a bitter and hopeless discovery. The dumb spirit dwelling in the sick person is stronger. The scribes already knew that, and we can easily guess what they were saying: Who do you think you are? As if you were able to overcome sickness! That's the way it is. Jesus' friends are discouraged, as it often happened with them. What does it mean when a person is really a Christian but in reality is not stronger than other people! And Jesus doesn't offer any consolation to the disciples; he doesn't say: It will happen, be patient! But he confronts them: What a bunch of sad sacks, how long do I have to put up with you?

Why are the disciples so backward, so faithless, as it says in the text, so off the mark? Because they cannot believe that all things are possible. All things are possible to him who believes. To be a human being is more than just adapting to the circumstances. To be a human being means to say that *all things are possible.* The world can be free of nuclear weapons and of hunger. The sick boy can be healthy. There is enough work for every person. There is work that does not make us duller, more exhausted, and spiritually and intellectually poorer. There is good work to be had which enriches us and is meaningful for others and for ourselves. All things are possible—that is a sentence for which we need faith.

Faith is an important word in the story of Jesus and in the Bible. Without faith you can't live authentically; you can't ever really become a human being. Without faith you say to yourself: that can't happen—there is nothing more to expect. The young man who talked about assembly-line work had something in mind other than what was being done with the young women who were his colleagues. Behind his words we can hear his dream, his faith. You cannot live authentically without trusting that life is good, even your life, that the difficulties and setbacks are not the last word, not even for you, and that your life has a purpose.

In the story from Mark 9 Jesus addresses the father because the father also is fixed on the "practical realities." If you can! says Jesus. What a question! Whoever believes can do anything! Perhaps he also said to the father: If you have a purpose in life that your son can recognize and that he can help you with, then all things are possible. Maybe Jesus simply asked the father: And what are you living for? And when the father then had to admit that he was living only for money and had nothing else in mind and that his son just wasn't suited for this life, then it became clearer why the father could be of no help to the boy.

Without faith our life can go only as far as we are able to see right now. We won't be able to see beyond the fact that the boy is sick and had attempted suicide because his life appeared to be so meaningless.

Faith: All Things Are Possible

We need nuclear weapons in order to secure ourselves against the attacks of others, in order to avoid external coercion, and getting rid of them is impossible. "Where there is no vision the people perish" (Proverbs 29:18, Soelle/Steffensky).

To have faith means to have a vision. Not just a private dream that someone has all by himself, but a big dream that we can all dream together.

A hymn: *We're Having a Dream* *

CONGREGATION: We're having a dream
And when everyone laughs,
We'll have a dream
Of a better world.

CANTOR: There the streets aren't traffic-clogged,
There the air is suddenly clean,
There the plants aren't lead-polluted,
And life is beautiful there.

CONGREGATION: We're having a dream . . .

CANTOR: There everyone receives what he needs,
There everyone needs what he receives,
There no person is unemployed,
And life is beautiful there.

CONGREGATION: We're having a dream . . .

CANTOR: There work brings us satisfaction again,
There the goods are quality goods,
There you're able to repair them yourselves,
And life is beautiful there.

CONGREGATION: We're having a dream . . .

CANTOR: There no one dictates what we should do,
There I myself sing my very own song,
There I sing songs with others as well,
And life is beautiful there.

CONGREGATION: We're having a dream. . . .
And giving it life,
We're having a dream
And creating a new world.

*From *Anfänge neuen Lebens, Gottesdienst in der Katharinenkirche in Hamburg*, 1978 (*Beginnings of a New Life, Worship in the Church of St. Catharine in Hamburg*), based on a text by Günter Hildebrandt, *Wir träumen einen Traum* © 1975 by Peter Janssens Musik Verlag, Telgte.

Not Just Yes and Amen

CANTOR: There self-determination is real,
There citizens help citizens themselves,
There one is no longer alone
And life is beautiful there.

CONGREGATION: We're having a dream
And giving it life,
We're having a dream
And creating a new world.

Church: They Had Everything in Common

A man whose wife died recently and left him with two children said to us:

> I often don't know how it can go on like this, with my job and with the two small children. But I'll make it. I don't need help from anyone. I don't want to be a burden to anyone. When I can't get myself to go on any longer, I just take some Valium. No one really cares how I am or how I'm making out. I don't show anyone how I'm feeling inside. Since the first day after my wife died I've told my kids that they don't have to alter their lives in any way. The children should not have to suffer for the fact that my wife is dead. And our grief is our own business and no one else's.

At first we marveled about this man. He was strong. He didn't bewail his fate. He was managing two jobs (his work and his kids). He didn't bother anyone else. But then we began to ask whether it really was desirable and human to be so strong and independent. Why should he conceal his pain? Isn't it more human to show it and to allow others to share it? Is it really true that no one cares about how he lives his life? Aren't we here mutually to look after each other's hurts and to share our burdens? Isn't he asking too much of himself to want to be outwardly as strong as a giant? His behavior is certainly consistent with one of the popular rules of our society which people often cynically express: God helps those who help themselves?

There is a story in the New Testament that speaks against this:

> Now the company of those who believed were of one heart and soul, and no one said that any of the things which he possessed was his own, but they had everything in common. And with great power the apostles

gave their testimony to the resurrection of the Lord Jesus, and great grace was upon them all. There was not a needy person among them, for as many as were possessors of lands or houses sold them, and brought the proceeds of what was sold and laid it at the apostles' feet; and distribution was made to each as any had need.

Acts 4:32–35

In that young church and among those new Christians there was no one who owned something and kept it for himself alone. Possessions were sold, and the money was distributed according to individual need. No one was ashamed to accept something. Their slogan was not, *God helps those who help themselves*. Rather, because God helps everyone, they were there to help each other. That is the church—or better said, that is what the church should be; each one for everyone.

Throughout the world today in the midst of a paralyzed church life, new groups of base communities are being established. These are groups of people who want to live together as Christians. They share their free time, often their possessions, and share the tasks which they commit themselves to in their part of the city, in their neighborhoods. The starting point of this activity is not in the work of pastors but is *based* in the work of ordinary people. Pastors and priests are coworkers like all the others. The people in these base communities often have difficulties with the official church, because in their prayers and in their celebrations they are not being just *purely religious* but are very consciously there for the poor and underprivileged. Whenever they make efforts to offer tutoring help to Turkish schoolchildren who don't know the German language, they always run up against difficulties: with their church authorities, with the neighbors who complain that they're making too much noise, and often with public officials as well. All this means, however, that the members of the base community grow even closer together and help each other out: with cooking the meals, with child care, with traveling long distances to an office or to a doctor. They live less and less for themselves alone. They become more and more the church, not because they are being more churchly, but because they are taking the gospel more seriously.

John, the forerunner of Jesus, was asked: "What should we do then?" He answered: "Whoever has two coats, share with the one who has none; and whoever has food, do likewise" (Luke 3:11, Soelle/Steffensky).

The people to whom John said that were extremely poor. The tattered and the half-naked were no exceptions. Our difficulty today is that the poor are so far from us and are known to us only indirectly via television, newspapers, and books. In spite of this we think that the church, today as well as back then, begins with one thing: sharing.

Maybe in reality it wasn't completely that way for the first Christians. But, in this story about the early church, every church of today now has a picture by which it must let itself be measured and by which it can show whether it is really *church*.

The early Christians were of one heart and soul, as it says in the text from Acts. Other passages of the Bible express this close fellowship of Christians in a similar way. Several times it says that the whole church is one body with many members. When one of these members suffers, says 1 Corinthians (12:26), then all the members suffer; when one member rejoices, then all the members rejoice. We think again of the man whose wife died and of his loneliness. He is proud and independent. But no one is there to share his grief. He wants to weep with no one. When he is weak, he wants to show it to no one. He would rather swallow some Valium. The French writer Paul Valery once said: "Alone we are always in bad company." Alone we have less courage and strength for living. Alone we run right up against our anxiety. Alone we do not come up with many new ideas.

However, more belong to the church than those living in the present who share property and the potentialities of life with each other and are *one in heart and soul*. To the church belong also all those who have lived before us and who have been attached to the meaning which faith in Jesus gives to life. To the church belong also those who have died. Church is the place where the dead are not forgotten and where their stories continue to be told. We would like to tell the story of one of those who have died, namely Dietrich Bonhoeffer, and then we'll say why it's important to remember him. Bonhoeffer (1906–1945) was an important figure in the church's struggle against the Nazis. From the very beginning he fought against

Dietrich Bonhoeffer (1906–1945)

Church: They Had Everything in Common

National Socialism and against the pastors and theologians who fell into it. He organized and directed a seminary for young theologians of the Confessing Church. The Confessing Church was that part of the church that was least deceived by Nazi ideology. For that reason, and because he interceded for persecuted Jews, the Nazis made things difficult for him. His situation became increasingly untenable. He was not allowed to speak in public or to publish his writings. Friends of Bonhoeffer who wanted to protect him were able to get him a teaching position in theology in New York City. That was in 1939, shortly before the outbreak of the war. "Stay here," his American friends said to him. "You can help people in Germany far better from here than if you were over there."

Bonhoeffer hesitated for a long time and did not know what to do. He wrote to a colleague in New York:

> I have come to the conclusion that I have made a mistake in coming to America. I must live through this difficult period in our national history alongside Christians in Germany. I can have no right to reconstruct Christian life in Germany after the war if I do not share in the trials of this period along with my people. My brothers in the Synod of the Confessing Church decided that I should get away. It may be that they were right when they urged me to do so; but it was wrong on my part to leave. Such a decision every person has to make for himself. Christians in Germany now stand before the frightful alternative of either willing the defeat of their own nation so that Christian civilization can live on, or to speak out for victory, which will eventually destroy civilization. I know which of these alternatives I have to choose, but I cannot make this choice while I remain in safety.

Bonhoeffer did not want to shrink from the confrontations, from the struggle, nor even from his possible death. He went back and was active in the political resistance with those who on 20 July 1944 attempted to assassinate Hitler. In 1943 he was imprisoned and a few days before the end of the war he was hanged by the Nazis in the Flossenburg concentration camp.

What does it mean to know the story of this man who is now dead? One person out of the community to which we belong, a Christian, had a big dream in life. He thought that human dignity belonged to everyone, also to Jews, also to gypsies. He committed himself to this dream, which at that time seemed impossible and was mortally dangerous. He did not choose the expected way out, to remain in safety in America, but he returned to Germany, even though that return cost him his life. This decisive moment in his life touches us almost more than his death in the concentration camp: he gave up his security and chose the struggle against fascist murder and death. It strengthens our faith in life when we can see how a person lived his life without betraying himself. The dream that we have for our lives will then be clearer, more radical, sharper, when we take seriously how grand and how courageous the dream of this departed person really was. We shall also feel that we owe something to this one person who died, namely to embody a portion of what he dreamed. The one who died needs us, because his grand desires for this life are not yet fulfilled. We must keep the flame burning, the flame that he began. Church—that is, the potentialities of our life—resides not in us alone; we have brothers and sisters who help us in life; we have fathers and mothers; we have the deceased, whose successful lives encourage and strengthen us. When we are too weak by ourselves to preserve life's grand desires and dreams, we can look for the dreams which our fellow Christians of the past have had. Precisely because we recognize that our own lives, isolated and separated from others, are barren and insufficient, we have therefore linked ourselves up with the desires, the courage, and the work of the many. We discover then, that we certainly don't need to be alone and live for ourselves only. There were people before us who have engaged in the struggle. There once was this Dietrich Bonhoeffer who did not remain in the safety of America, and his courage was brought back home. Again and again there have always been groups of people who were capable of resistance. When the Nazis decreed that every Jew had to wear a yellow star with the word "Jew" printed on it, the Danish king and many people in Denmark along with him declared: "Then we all shall wear such a star!"

Church means also to have a place where such stories are remembered and told. We need these risky memories of the many and the courageous who are around us and have gone before us. We also need to have confidence in those who will come after us. We hope that when our own strength diminishes those who come after us will achieve more than we have achieved. As the farmers who were over-come in their struggle for liberation from the princes sang:

Returning
We come home defeated
But our grandchildren will win
If it's ever repeated

When a person grows old in dignity he then learns that it doesn't matter whether he has won every victory by himself alone. It sounds old-fashioned but it is very true: it's comforting to know that we don't have to do everything alone and that our failures do not mean the failure of the cause for which we have fought. That is *church*: that we are never alone, never alone in our dreaming, never alone in our defeats.

Eternal Life: To Remain in Love

I know a woman in Hamburg who has been living alone for five years. At the end of the war she fled from Pomerania to Hamburg. Since her husband died she has been renting out two rooms of her apartment in order to increase her own income. The only people she knows are the renters and the neighbors who live on her floor. They don't want to have children, she says.

Her life consists in keeping the apartment in order, going to market (often for the renters as well), and cooking. She cooks only for herself. Afternoons she watches television. She reads seldom, a magazine every now and then. It is not easy to converse with her; she always tells the same jokes. She is most lively when she can talk about how it used to be in Pomerania, her life in the country, her job. But her powers of recollection are weak; she seldom speaks of anything other than herself; she knows nothing about her grandparents. She is not religiously active. Through her confirmation instruction she came in touch only superficially with Christianity, but it doesn't mean much to her, neither for her personally nor for the very small world in which she is living her life. When she was driven from her homeland what remained of religion in her simply atrophied.

"Everyone has his job to do," she says. She measures herself over against others: whoever scrubs, goes shopping, or does this or that. She has become friendly with a former colleague at work.

"But I don't let her in the house," she said to me. Her livingroom is always spotless. She knows where you can get the tastiest sausage for the cheapest price. She has some health concerns, about her own body, of course. When one of the neighborhood boys had a fatal accident on his motorcycle, she observed: "And his parents put a lot of money into that boy."

I've told the story of this woman because I want to say something about death. About the very normal death of a meaningless life. A life with no connection to other human beings, with no participation with them, without her making any difference in anyone else's lives. The Bible speaks out against this kind of a very normal life. It doesn't even call it living; it calls it being dead. "Whoever is not there for others is dead" (1 John 3:14, Soelle/ Steffensky). Or in an older translation: "Whoever does not love the brother remains in death."

Many people are dead, even though they're still walking around. At one time or another they begin to forget about living, about the will to live, about the inner feeling of rage, about that great heartbeat when one falls in love, about the fear that something terrible is about to happen, about the dream of a future.

The Bible says that anyone who lives without a relationship to others is as good as dead. The Bible has a beautiful and rich conception about authentic life, fulfilled life:

> Let us live for one another, for living for another comes from God and corresponds to his life. Whoever lives for others is born of God and knows him, whoever does not live for others does not know God. For God is living for others.
> No person has ever seen God, but when we live for one another we participate in God's life, and his life for us will be perfected in us.
> 1 John 4:7–8, 12 (Soelle-Steffensky)

God is love—that is the simplest, most beautiful, and clearest thing we can say about God. The one who loves and has relationships with others comes out of the state of being dead. Religion is another word for relationship. Originally it meant to bind, to rebind. The one who is bound together with others, with the creation, and also with himself, his own desires and dreams, is the one we call *religious*.

Many New Testament stories about the infirm tell how people have *died* through their sickness because they could not really live with others. In Jerusalem near the sheep's gate there is a pool named Bethesda whose water was supposed to have healing power. From time to time it was supposed to move; an angel came down and moved it. The one who was the first to get into the water after it moved would be healed. But many, many infirm, lame, blind, leprous people waited year round for the miracle.

> One man was there, who had been ill for thirty-eight years. When Jesus saw him and knew that he had been lying there for a long time, he said to him, "Do you want to be healed?" The sick man answered him, "Sir, I have no man to put me into the pool when the water is troubled, and while I am going another steps down before me." Jesus said to him, "Rise, take up your pallet, and walk." And at once the man was healed, and he took up his pallet and walked. Now that day was the sabbath.
>
> John 5:5–9

The most pathetic sentence in this story is: "Sir, I have no one!" In that sentence lies all the misery of a thirty-year-old sickness. The man is alone, helpless, and condemned forever to be sick. Without other people he has no chance. But the sick person must still have some hope. Otherwise he wouldn't turn to Jesus. He wouldn't answer at all.

The woman in Hamburg doesn't even have that. She isn't waiting for an angel to move the water. She tells no one how empty her life is. Not even herself. She can neither ask nor pray.

We often think that sickness is something connected only to the body and that therefore the healing must happen to the body. But in the New Testament all sicknesses and infirmities are seen for what they really are: social sicknesses. They have something to do with the society in which one lives. Sickness is not a private matter of one individual, which he or she must work out alone. Every sickness contains a question directed to other people. Those who have a nervous breakdown or are in an emotional crisis conceal it from their employers and colleagues. They thereby intensify their loneliness. Recently I met an African who was doing very well in Germany. He was earning a decent salary. "But one thing I don't want to do in Germany: grow old. That must be terrible."

An older person, a human being, who no longer produces according to expectations must then say: Sir, I have no one to put me into the pool. There is no hope. He is left alone and then the sickness gains strength and worsens. To be healed in the sense of Jesus means no longer to have to say: I have no one.

When a person comes out of the death in which he finds himself and into life, we call it *eternal life*. We can also say: authentic life, or happiness, or life that no longer separates us and cuts us off from the great life which we call God.

Many people think that eternal life comes only after we die. But the Bible holds it to be much nearer to us. Jesus lived that life—and his friends do also.

> Being asked by the Pharisees when the kingdom of God was coming, he answered them, "The kingdom of God is not coming with signs to be observed; nor will they say, 'Lo, here it is!' or 'There!' for behold, the kingdom of God is in the midst of you."
>
> Luke 17:20–21

Eternal life is not an endlessly long period of something that we already know, nor a quantitative idea, but something different and new, a qualitative idea. "You are my friends if you do what I command you. . . . This I command you, to love one another" (John 15:14, 17).

Recently a young girl asked me in a discussion: "At death is it all over?" I wanted to know what was behind her question. Was she talking about herself? Was she perhaps afraid of getting cancer and having to die? Or did she ask because she had lost a girlfriend or boyfriend and was looking for some kind of consolation in the hope of their seeing each other again after this life? Or was it more of a theoretical question that you often get in a discussion? I had been trying to talk about *eternal life* as it occurs here on earth. Most of the time the Bible doesn't use the word "dead" in the biological sense, but rather as if we said about something: It's all over! Forget it! I thought for a long time about what I could say to this young girl. Finally I replied: when we say "At death it's all over," it depends on what we mean by the word *all*. If, when you say *all*, you never mean anything more than yourself, then, as far as you're concerned, at death it's all over. If, however, your life includes everything that is around you, when you are a part of the total life of the earth, a part of that love which binds together human beings with the creation, then you know for sure that after you die it is not all over. It goes on; it continues. Then you have become a part of the life process. Then you have become the water of life as well. Then nothing is over, because *God is not over.*

Kingdom of God: Freedom from Having, Freedom for Living

We used to live near Cologne and had a neighbor whose wife had died. They had no children and were very much attached to their possessions. One day he had his house plastered and one of our children leaned his bicycle against one of the walls of his house. The neighbor came over and took us outside to see, and then he said angrily: "Look! See this! This mark!" And then he said something also with a much sadder voice: "It's on my property, and my property is the only thing I still have."

I'll never forget that statement. It was actually the only thing my neighbor had: his house, his garden, his land. Property. It had to be protected against noise and dirt and children and other pesky people. He himself was sad that things had gotten to that point for him, but that didn't help much now. His life was based on what he had, on the having. This desire is there in everyone: to make life more secure through what we have. If you have something then you are something. Is that true? What does it mean that *you are something*, what does it mean *to be something*?

The Bible constantly warns against riches. It is Jesus' opinion that life is not to be based on having, buying, getting, possessing, consuming. What is the most important thing for you? What are you living for?

There are also children and young people who try to build their lives on having. They buy friends, insist on their standards for them, speak disrespectfully about what others have (forget it!), bribe others with candy. But just as you can't buy life, neither can you buy friends. There are other important things in life: being helpful, being rich in ideas, having a sense of humor, being reliable—these are important. What is decisive is not what one *has* but what one *is*.

Kingdom of God: Freedom from Having, Freedom for Living

It isn't hard to tell the difference between people, whether they are *dead* because they're interested only in things like bank accounts, cars, or houses, or whether they have given a different meaning to their lives. It often happens that we meet a person who by the look on his face tells us that he's alive. His life has direction, a goal. As long as you think that happiness consists in having and getting more, as long as you are dependent on things, you are not yet free. Jesus talked a lot about that.

> Don't lay up for yourselves treasures on earth, for moths and worms, burglars and thieves. Make God your treasure whom neither moths nor worms can erode, neither thieves nor burglars can rob. Think of this: where your treasure is, there will your heart be also.
>
> Matthew 6:19–21 (Soelle-Steffensky)

As this criticism is directed against rich people, we must not think only of millionaires. It is meant for every person who lives for money. Where our treasure is—there, what we work for, what we're concerned about, what we dream about, will our heart be also. In Jesus' opinion rich people are all those whose most important interest in life is money. At a senior-high-school-class gathering all the candidates for graduation were asked what they wanted to be later in life. After a long silence, a young man stood up and said that he really didn't know yet, but one thing was clear: it better pay well. Several of the parents laughed embarrassingly as if it were a bit improper to say something like that so directly. But he was only repeating what he had learned for nineteen years.

The Bible speaks out:

1. against property and against people who have fallen under its spell;
2. against the domination of people by people who think riches get them the right to have the last word;
3. against institutions, such as factories or businesses, school or church, courtroom or hospital, which function according to the same basic pattern: according to what you have and not according to what you are.

The first Christians were persecuted because they were not so concerned about having property and because they had enough of that ruling authority which only protected injustice, and because they could not participate in many of the established institutions, such as temple service, military service, devotion to the emperor. Today black Christians in South Africa, the *campesinos* in South America, the female workers in the electronics industry in the Philippines are all impoverished and oppressed. They often assemble together to organize their activity, to pray together, and to read the Bible. Even that is—for example, in El Salvador—a crime. There the Bible is something *subversive*. It is a forbidden and dangerous book. When pastors read this book together with the poor and the police are listening, it happens again and again that a few days later the priest disappears or for some unexplained reasons is run over by a motorcycle or simply found dead. Perhaps the priest had read something like this to his people:

> Their hands are upon what is evil, to do it diligently; the prince and the judge ask for a bribe, and the great man utters the evil desire of his soul; thus they weave it together.
>
> Micah 7:3

Or words like these from the prophet Ezekiel:

> Her princes in the midst of her are like a roaring lion tearing the prey; they have devoured human lives; they have taken treasure and precious things; they have made many widows in the midst of her.
>
> Ezekiel 22:25

This criticism of the rulers should not result in the poor becoming rulers themselves or in the rulers themselves becoming fat on the allures of kingship. Jesus criticized rulership radically, not only for certain others but for everyone:

> And Jesus called them to him and said to them, "You know that those who are supposed to rule over the Gentiles lord it over them, and their great men exercise authority over them. But it shall not be so among you; but whoever would be great among you must be your servant, and whoever would be first among you must be slave of all. For the Son of man also came not to be served but to serve, and to give his life as a ransom for many."
>
> Mark 10:42–45

Often we are caught or enslaved because we have gotten ourselves into certain alliances and thereby have gotten ourselves into the position of being ruled over. Whoever has to pay for a house allows his employer to do anything he wants. The one who worries about losing his job is going to put up with even more. The one who wants good grades will do his bowing before the teacher.

The Bible points to another way which does not allow us to be less free, more fearful, and more cowardly but does allow us to be more courageous and stronger. That means that our ideas about what is especially important to us must be arranged accordingly.

> I tell you:
> Do not be anxious about the things you need for life, for food, for clothing. Isn't life more than food and drinks and the body more than clothing?
> Look at the birds of the air, they neither sow nor reap, nor do they gather into barns. In spite of this God provides for them, and certainly also for you first as well.
> And don't worry yourselves silly unnecessarily, you can't lengthen your life one bit.
> Why do you fret about clothing? Look at the flowers, how they grow; they neither toil nor spin, but I say to you: Not even Solomon in all his glory was as beautiful as one of these flowers that grows wild in the field. Today they shoot up, already tomorrow they are burned up. In spite of this God clothes them, and certainly does the same for you first as well.
> You trust him too little, and it is precisely you who must no longer ask yourselves: How will we get our food, our clothing? Let that be asked by those people who know nothing of God. You are his sons and daughters; he knows that you need all these things. He it is who creates justice in the land, and that is what you should be concerned about first of all; everything else will take care of itself.
>
> Matthew 6:25–33/Luke 12:22–31
> (Soelle-Steffensky)

The last two verses are rendered in Luther's translation: "Aim first for the Kingdom of God and everything else will fall to you as well."

If we really understand these words and then try to live according to them, we shall experience a great liberation. If the issue is justice, our fear and our false hesitancy will fade. It will no longer disturb me when I appear ridiculous to other people. I no longer ask: What does this look like? God is behind me like an invisible wall for me to lean against. Others see only me and find what I do rather useless, but those who have found that great liberation of living for what is important to them will be, as Martin Luther put it, "a free lord over all things and subject to no one."

In early 1982 there was a great deal of concern over the issue of food in Poland. Therefore, a few people in Cologne had the following idea: on Saturdays they stood at the entrance to a big supermarket at the peak shopping period and distributed to those who went into the store flyers requesting assistance for Poland. People were asked to purchase something that could then be sent to Poland: powdered milk, lard, a can of sausage, and so forth.

Our friends in Cologne did this in two different places and were speechless over what they experienced. People from the working-class neighborhoods of Cologne-Ehrenfeld almost without exception purchased something for them to send, some contributing just a pound of sugar, some contributing more. In no time they had filled a whole truck with provisions. On the other hand, people in a higher class neighborhood reacted differently. They either wouldn't take the flyers or they put them away quickly without reading them. Many started to discuss the issue and said that the Poles didn't want to work and that it was all their own fault. Only a few contributed any food, even though individually they gave more. The total provisions received were much less than what the poorer people contributed.

There are many ways to learn sharing. Powdered milk for Polish children has something to do with the kingdom of God.

I know some young people who stand every Friday evening at a certain place and observe a period of "silence for peace." They do nothing but stand there silently. They have flyers with them explaining why they are against the continuing arms buildup in our country. That too is sharing. It is sharing concern about the future, sharing knowledge, keeping informed, doing one's part. To enlighten others and to get them to take part in learning who is pushing us closer to war. The statements of our politicians provide little information on the question. The young people have told me their experiences when they engage in these periods of silence: Many people look ardently in another direction, many quicken their steps. Many stand there and yell profanities at the young people, curse them out or start to laugh at them. That's not easy to take.

Cross: The Cry of the Tortured

I want to tell the story of Steve Biko, an African resistance fighter, who was born in 1946 in King Williams Town in the Union of South Africa. As a student in a black college he was accepted into medical school, a highly uncommon achievement. He became involved quite early in the student movement that advocated equality for all so-called colored schoolchildren. Such children went to school in totally overcrowded classrooms where poorly educated teachers did more baby-sitting than teaching. Steve Biko was a freedom fighter.

One day in Durham Steve Biko met a man who worked as a delivery-truck driver for a dry-cleaning firm. He spoke of his daily routine: he got up at 4:00 a.m., and after a long walk he took a bus to town, where as an Asian Indian he was not allowed to live. That is a rule of the apartheid system, by which people of color are kept *apart* from whites. After a long day at work he had to count on another three hours getting home, arriving there at 9:30 p.m., too tired to do anything else but sleep. The next day it was the same thing all over again. This man said to Steve: "I don't work any more in order to live; I live in order to work."

That's the way it is with millions of people in South Africa. That is the reality of apartheid, and this man was still lucky that he could live with his family. The majority of black workers have to leave their families far away in the homelands and can visit their wives and children only once a year.

Steve Biko saw the greatest misfortune of his compatriots to be the inner oppression caused by external exploitation. Together with others he attempted to awaken the consciousness of black people by means of the Black Consciousness Movement (BCM):

Steve Biko (1946 – 1977)

I believe that the black person in this country is suppressed by two strong elements. First he is oppressed by the external world of institutionalized machinery, by laws which forbid him to do certain things, by poor working conditions, meager wages, very difficult living conditions, and a miserable education. All this comes to him from the outside. Second, and most important for us, the black person has developed a certain condition of alienation within himself; he negates himself because he connects everything good with *white*. In other words, when he thinks of something good and beautiful, he immediately thinks of the white people who experience such things. This comes from the black person's way of life and originates from his childhood development.

So black people despise and hate themselves. That is something the white overlords have taught them to do.

Steve Biko became a revolutionary who wanted to give back to people their dignity and self-respect, as well as their consciousness.

We are trying to bring black people to the point of dealing realistically with their problems and trying to find solutions, so that they can be able to develop something called a consciousness, a physical consciousness of their situation and are able to answer for themselves. The intention behind this is to make way for a kind of hope. . . . Human beings should not surrender to the hardships of life. Human beings must develop hope.

For the white rulers in South Africa this program, with its goals of a change of heart, of hope, and of consciousness, was too dangerous. Like so many black leaders, Steve Biko was *banned*, which is another feature of the apartheid system: the banned person is not allowed to travel, to be on the street after dark, to speak with more than one person at a time, and he must report once a week to the police. Steve was a lively, vital, strong person. He loved, drank, and liked to joke with his friends; he enjoyed it when they were able to outfox the police who shadowed him, and even as a banned person he continued to work in the movement.

The liberation that he wanted was also to be for the benefit of the white oppressors. His goal was a country free of racism and reconciliation between the races. In September of 1977 he was imprisoned. The police tortured and beat him. Naked and without medical attention, he was brought to a prison hospital almost five hundred miles away from where he was imprisoned. There he died. With him died also the great hope of many white South Africans who are not racists and who were hoping for a peaceful solution to the problem.

Biko had a friend, a clergyman from England, who called him a "selfless revolutionary." In this case "selfless" means that Steve was totally free from hate, bitterness, or prejudice. The humiliations never caused him to lose his *ubuntu*, his humanity. As he was being tortured, when he was already doomed to die because of a fractured skull, he told one of the guards who brought him some water that he would like to kiss him.

To remember a martyr like Steve Biko is to allow oneself also to remember one's own humanity. By humanity we do not mean the ability just calmly to observe the things that are going on around us. Humanity means: involvement, solidarity with the oppressed, and resistance against the oppressor. To humanity belong struggle and suffering. That is expressed in the Christian tradition with a very simple sign, which everyone can write by hand in the air. That sign is the cross, and it speaks of selfless, revolutionary love. Originally the cross was simply an instrument of torture by which the Roman state would slowly and painfully execute insurrectionists and poor runaway slaves. Crucify him! meant as much as: let him be tortured to death.

Just as today people are tortured for hours by means of electronic instruments—like those who, after losing consciousness, have water splashed on them and then are again hooked up to the machine—so it happened to Jesus of Nazareth, who was seen as a dangerous person, a terrorist, a subversive, an anarchist, and an agitator.

> Two others also, who were criminals, were led away to be put to death with him. And when they came to the place which is called The Skull, there they crucified him, and the criminals, one on the right and one on the left. And Jesus said, "Father, forgive them; for they know not what they do." And they cast lots to divide his garments. And the people stood by, watching; but the rulers scoffed at him, saying, "He saved others; let him save himself, if he is the Christ of God, his Chosen One!" The soldiers also mocked him, coming up and offering him vinegar, and saying, "If you are the King of the Jews, save yourself!" There was also an inscription over him, "This is the King of the Jews."
> One of the criminals who were hanged railed at him, saying, "Are you

not the Christ? Save yourself and us!" But the other rebuked him, saying, "Do you not fear God, since you are under the same sentence of condemnation? And we indeed justly; for we are receiving the due reward of our deeds; but this man has done nothing wrong." And he said, "Jesus, remember me when you come into your kingdom." And he said to him, "Truly, I say to you, today you will be with me in Paradise."

It was now about the sixth hour, and there was darkness over the whole land until the ninth hour, while the sun's light failed; and the curtain of the temple was torn in two. Then Jesus, crying with a loud voice, said, "Father, into thy hands I commit my spirit!" And having said this he breathed his last. Now when the centurion saw what had taken place, he praised God, and said, "Certainly this man was innocent!"

Luke 23:32–47

Before this crucifixion Jesus was beaten and mocked. "Save yourself!" "If you were able to help others, why don't you help yourself?" Such oft-repeated epithets are a kind of psychological torture. Today it has its counterpart in the way prisoners are told that their comrades have already confessed and that they should therefore give up their pointless resistance. But Jesus did not help himself out by retracting his statements or submitting to the ruling powers. He remained a selfless revolutionary who was faithful also to those who tortured him to death. He prayed for their forgiveness, for they knew not what they were doing.

I used to understand the story of Jesus' crucifixion as the terrible, tragic end of a great idealistic person. I noticed how alone Jesus was after his friends like Judas forsook him, how Peter had denied him, and how on one occasion his three best friends simply went to sleep when he really needed them. He had hundreds of spectators, but he was always alone. So much so that he finally felt forsaken by God as well. "My God, my God, why have you forsaken me?" he prayed, with the words of an old psalm. Then he cried aloud and died. So it is told by the ancient evangelists.

Today I think a bit differently, because I have learned much from the martyrs of our century. Martin Luther King, Jr., Dietrich Bonhoeffer, Ita Ford, Oscar Romero, Maximilian Kolbe, Steve Biko . . . to name only a few. When I read of their deaths, I find pieces of life, of ongoing, indestructible life. I see in the dead ones and in their dying something that transcends the tragedy, that is more than a despairing cry to God. God is here, also in the dying. In the biblical story such signs of life are there even in death, even during torture: when Jesus prays for his murderers; when he promises life to the one criminal who turned to him; and finally when the centurion standing there only as an observer suddenly sees the truth.

In Jesus' death the life, the way, the truth is not extinguished or surrendered, as if everything had no meaning any more. We say that nothing has meaning only when we do not believe in the way, the truth, and the life. When believing means that we love selflessly, then this love is still to be seen also in dying. And just as the members of the ancient church exclaimed to each other: "Jesus lives! He is risen!" so people of today exclaim: Steve Biko Lives! Oscar Romero lives! Jesus of Nazareth lives! Love does not die.

God: Nothing Is Lost

It's difficult for us to put our faith in God into words and to communicate it to others. There are many reasons for this. One of them is that we would have to talk about something that affects us personally. Another is the frivolous way that many Christians and theologians talk about God, making faith in God more impossible than possible. For example: we were at the funeral of a young man who had died of cancer. His mother was weeping and wailing at the graveside and was really out of her mind. Afterward, the minister who buried the man said coldheartedly: "If you really believe, you don't have to cry. This mother must know that her son is with God."

This scene made the impression on us that the preaching of the Word of God can serve to trivialize people's pain and to disregard it.

The most important reason that we are able only with difficulty to talk about God is that we cannot believe in him without doubting. By doubting we understand primarily the trouble it takes to harmonize biblical statements with one's intellect and with a modern world view. Isn't *God* only a helpless attempt from a prescientific era to explain natural phenomena which as yet have no explanation?

This kind of doubting, however, is not what occupies us the most. Far more than an enlightened intellect, what bothers us most are the questions: Where was God at Auschwitz? Where was he when the children in Vietnam were burned with napalm? Where is he when people are tortured in South Africa? Where is he when young people die of cancer? Why does he remain silent when we can hardly endure living?

In his book *The Last of the Just* the French author Andre Schwarz-Bart describes a discussion between the Jewish laundryman Goldfaden and his apprentice Benjamin. Goldfaden is old and tired of living. He is about to be fired because he can hardly hold the pressing iron any more, and he confesses to Benjamin that he no longer believes in God.

> "But look, Mr. Goldfaden," said Benjamin, numb with terror.
> "If there were no God, what would we be then, you and I?"
> "Poor little Jewish workers, right?"
> "Is that all?"
> "Unfortunately," said the old laundryman.
> The next night, lying on a straw mattress, Benjamin tried to envision things as Mr. Goldfaden saw them. One thing led to another, and he came to the startling conclusion that Zemyock (his hometown) was only a ridiculously tiny piece of the universe if it were true that God did not exist. But, he asked himself, what then would be the purpose of all the suffering? And, seeing Mr. Goldfaden's despairing expression before him, he shouted with a deep sob that tore through the darkness of the workshop: *"Everything is lost, oh, my God, everything is lost!"*

That's all! We can't believe in God, and we can have no hope in life! This notion was arrived at by the old laundryman not after lengthy deliberation but after a long and worrisome life as a poor and exploited Jewish laborer. Protesting against faith in God does not come primarily from our enlightened intellect but from the humiliations that one has to put up with in life in the experience of destruction, of injustice, and of a daily existence which is hard to bear. Mr. Goldfaden had good and tangible experiences and arguments for his lack of faith: all the injustice, all the murder, and all the meaninglessness that has gone on and is still going on. One single tortured human being contradicts the meaning of the world. That is our doubt. Our faith in God has a flaw.

That's the way it is, but we can't satisfy ourselves that that is all there is to it. Later, as the apprentice Benjamin returned to his hometown and observed the faith and piety of its Jewish residents, he said: "My God, if this is all a mistake, I prefer it to the small truths of unbelief."

Two answers: Mr. Goldfaden says, we can't have faith. We must be satisfied with the hard, cold facts of reality and truth! That's the way the world is! And there's nothing more to say! Benjamin says, I shall rebel with my faith in God against this naked truth. Precisely because reality as it is does not satisfy me, therefore I *must* believe in God. If I lose my faith in God then I am in agreement with death.

With all our doubts and with our attempts to live with them we have learned that one must try to speak. One also must find a language for those about which there is really nothing more to say other than they are broken, killed, tormented, and despised.

We have to quit being silent over things about which there is nothing to say!

In the Bible and in Christianity we have found a language that demands more of life than it gives. The blind see. The lame walk. The mourners are consoled. The hungry are fed. The dead live! This language we are glad to speak because it reminds us that we must never be satisfied with blindness, lameness, the tears of mourners, and the hunger of the have-nots. To believe in God means never to be satisfied with the mangled life; it also means to be willing to stand up for it and for life's wholeness.

What does the God in whom we are trying to believe look like, and where can we find him? The answer is something we as Christians cannot simply pull out of the air. Christians believe that there is a constant picture of God, namely in the form and life of Jesus of Nazareth and the stories and parables which he told about God. We recall one of these parables:

> When the Son of man appears as king
> he will say to the Just:
> I was hungry, and you gave me food;
> I was thirsty, you gave me drink;
> I was without civil rights, you received me in;
> I was naked, you gave me clothing;
> I was sick, you cared for me;
> I was in prison, you visited me there.
>
> For I tell you,
> What you have done for one of the least of
> my brothers and sisters,
> you have done for me.
>
> Matthew 25:34–40 (Soelle-Steffensky)

The story deals with a judgment that applies to all human beings.

The decisive question of the Judge will be how they have behaved toward him, toward this judging God.

But how could we behave at all toward you? ask the people who are judged. Have we ever seen you? Where could we find you? How could we talk to you and find out what you wanted? Where did you step forward with your mighty hosts to proclaim your divine will?

The Judge answers: I have cried out to you in the pleading of every single hungry person. My command reached you in the lament of every single prisoner. You did not need to look around very long. For I confronted you in the form of the tattered, the sick, the beaten, the alien and the foreign laborer, the homeless and the alcoholics.

This story about the form of God makes acceptable to us this God of whom we still have so many questions to ask. He stands on the side of life and especially on the side of those to whom life in its wholeness is denied and who do not reach the point of real living. He is not on the side of the rulers, the powerful, the rich, the affluent, the victorious. God takes sides with those who need him. He sides with the victims.

Resurrection: Mystery of Faith

We have already talked a lot about death and how people can be *dead* for forty years even though they bring home a salary, look stylish, and can manage nice vacation trips. We hope that it has become clear enough now what the Bible means by *dead.* It sounds pretty harsh when someone sitting across from you is called *dead.* The Bible is harsh, radical, and realistic, and it is able to see this death that is present everywhere; but it is never hopeless or cynical. The word "cynical" we can apply, for example, to people who are without hope for others and are of the opinion that they need no hope for themselves—that nothing makes any difference anyway. The Bible is not cynical when it describes the death that lurks around in life. Jesus once called the scribes "whited sepulchres."

> Woe to you, scribes and Pharisees, hypocrites! for you are like whitewashed tombs, which outwardly appear beautiful, but within they are full of dead men's bones and all uncleanness.
>
> Matthew 23:27

People can talk this way if they believe in resurrection. If they know: people can come back from being dead! They can begin to live again—no, not again, but to live, period!

I heard of a black Christian in Johannesburg, South Africa, by the name of Joe Mavi, who worked for the city as a bus driver. He was consumed with the truth that all people, even black people, are children of God whose dignity was being trampled on by the white racist minority government. He fought for justice, organized the city workers, and they elected him president of their labor union. He tells of how he fought for just wages, against unjust firings, and how he tried to achieve these goals through negotiations.

He was imprisoned five times, held in solitary confinement without being convicted. One of the times he was tortured he lost his hearing. He was constantly followed by the police and could not live any longer with his family. When friends of mine asked him how he could possibly go on living, he said: "It is not important whether I live or die. Dying is no sin. It is important that I now do what I need to do and what I can do."

Joe Mavi died on 8 June 1982 in an "automobile accident." Joe Mavi lived as a Christian, fought for God, and overcame death. The funeral service in the large Catholic church Regina Mundi in Soweto was filled to overflowing and was a testimony of faith in which the hope and determination of many people was strengthened to continue in solidarity the struggle for the gospel of peace.

Can it really be said that Joe Mavi is *dead*? Someone in a statistics bureau might be able to say that, but we really need a different, a human language. Joe Mavi is with those in Soweto who carry on his struggle. He is also with us wherever we take the side of the poor and participate in the great struggle for justice. Joe Mavi is not dead.

The people who lived together with Jesus were in a situation similar to that of black people in South Africa today. They had set their hopes on someone who was condemned to death. Was everything lost?

There are many different stories about the resurrection of Jesus. The Easter stories in the Bible tell of people who had become disillusioned and were without hope. The grave of Jesus is the place where they can do their remembering and where they can at least do their crying. But a young man stood at the entrance to the grave and asked the grieving women: Why do you seek the living among the dead?

There are several other mysterious stories about how the friends of Jesus again meet up with the one whom they thought was dead. One story deals with Mary Magdalene who went to the grave early in the morning. She stooped into the grave and saw sitting there two figures in white clothes; but Jesus whom she sought she did not find. Finally she saw a man whom she thought was the gardener. "Have you carried away my friend's body?" she asked this figure, and only when he answered her did she notice that it was Jesus.

Another story deals with two disciples walking toward Emmaus. On the way they met a stranger who noticed their sadness and talked with them about the hope in life which Jesus meant for them. It was only when they arrived at their destination and shared their bread with the stranger that they suddenly recognized who had been walking with them: it was the resurrected Jesus in another form.

A third example is in John's Gospel. Several disciples of Jesus had gone home after Jesus' death to the lake where they had previously lived as fishermen. They turned back to the old unpretentious life after the attempt at the great pretension had gone awry. One morning as they were fishing a stranger appeared on the shore. They didn't recognize him. Only when they began to share bread and fish with him did they suddenly notice that it was Jesus.

One can wonder why the resurrected Jesus appears in so many different forms: as a gardener, as a biblically literate traveler, as a stranger to the fishermen. He certainly did not come with a big shiny halo looking like a saint, which could make it clear to everyone: this is Jesus of Nazareth. He came enshrouded. He came incognito. He came to console his saddened friends—but they also had to be doing something in order to talk with him, and walk with him, and eat with him. Only then were they able to see that he was there. They couldn't get over it: this authentic life which he always talked about was there in that very moment. Indeed they could carry it on with each other. They no longer needed to wait in fear and trembling for their arrest. He lives—and for them that meant that we live also.

Resurrection is the mystery of faith. We do not understand mystery here in terms of a detective story which is no longer a mystery when we have figured it all out. This mystery is something that always remains a mystery, something we never completely and fully grasp. Resurrection means that Jesus comes to people in very different forms: as a beggar, as a gardener, as a crying child, as an old woman, as . . .

We can't predict it at all. But many thousands of Christians have discovered it and experienced it. Their lives, which looked dead, go on. They know very precisely through another person that it is there, in other people, that Jesus is not so easily done away with. They discover that they can hope. With each other we can break through the feeling that nothing goes right and that we can't do anything about it anyway. This experience with that Jesus who is risen and who comes into our lives is celebrated by us Christians at communion, or the Lord's Supper. We eat together and drink together in order to remember the mystery of faith: death does not have the last word. In faith in Christ we are united with the great hope and power of life.

Peace: God Disarms Unilaterally

The greatest calamity to happen in recent years is the new military arms buildup and the preparations for war. On 12 December 1979 the NATO leaders decided to submit to American pressure and to deploy new nuclear weapons in Europe, mainly in Germany. In Germany, in comparison with population and surface area, there already exist more nuclear weapons than in any comparable area in the entire world. So today still more and better weapons are being deployed, which can destroy Eastern Europe in about five minutes, that is, without appropriate warning time. Before this decision, which resulted from American pressure, there was an approximate balance of power between the two superpowers.

The American government, however, wants more than an approximate balance of power. It wants superiority. Even when it asserts that these measures will make peace more "secure," people in Europe ask why they will be more secure when they are able to kill every Russian eleven times over rather than only nine. And they are wondering who really gains from this security.

Since this decision by NATO a new, large movement for peace has arisen in all of Europe. People are simply afraid that what has already happened a thousand times in past history will be repeated: increased arms production leads to war. In Europe we have experienced this twice in the twentieth century alone. Both times Germans played a leading role: in the production of arms, in the deployment of weapons, in militarism, in the surprise attack on other countries, and finally in defeat. Increased arms production leads to war. Otherwise why should all these magnificent superaccurate weapons be produced if we really aren't going to use them?

The resistance against increased arms production is carried on by Christians in both East and West. We don't mean only a few admonitions toward peace like those we have heard from the pope or from the Protestant church in Germany. It is not enough to condemn nuclear war if we say nothing about its cause, the production of nuclear weapons. It is not enough to be against *arms production* in general if we do not make it clear who is pushing it, namely the West, and who is keeping up the pace, namely the East.

In the meantime, many churches have spoken out unequivocally against the possession, the testing, and the stockpiling of nuclear weapons. The Protestant church in Germany and the German Catholic Bishops Conference are not among them. They content themselves with generalizing statements like "We are for peace." The Dutch churches, the majority of the American Catholic bishops, the Reformed Church in Germany, and many individual congregations and Christians throughout the world are more consistent. They hold the opinion that the production of nuclear weapons is a sin in a threefold sense of the word. First, a sin against the Creator. God has created the world not so that we can destroy it—not even for testing purposes or in an "emergency." He has given us intelligence and inventive gifts not for the purpose of working toward mass murder. Our money and our mineral wealth and our energy are not there so that we can destroy the earth. If we were to carry out all the plans of the American military, we would have to destroy our land, our few recreation areas, our forests and water reserves simply to station poison gas and bombs over here. Even now, not just later, we are ruining the creation with this insanity.

Second, preparation for war is a sin against Jesus, who in traditional language is called *the Redeemer.* He has redeemed us from the enmity existing inside us, from that deathwish. When we keep arming ourselves we are like Cain. Whoever therefore always keeps playing Cain and keeps threatening other peoples, whoever still doesn't understand that Christ meets us in the hungering ones, for that person Jesus has died in vain. We cannot feed the poor with bombs; we need food for the world. The arms producers might call themselves Christians, but in reality they are working against Jesus when they advocate an arms production politics.

Third, preparation for war is a sin against the Holy Spirit. By *Holy Spirit* is meant that Spirit which drives out fear and which creates courage. Jesus promised *the Spirit* to his disciples when he had to leave them. He went to heaven, but sent the Spirit to his friends. The most important attributes of this Holy Spirit are that he spreads truth and creates courage. What does truth mean here? Christians don't have to be superexperts in order to understand what hunger is and what increased arms production means for the hungry. Every normal person on the street, even if he or she reads only the tabloids, can grasp that: millions for arms and next to nothing for the hungry! If this person should say: that's the way it's always been, you can't do anything about it, then the Spirit that brings truth and courage is not in him or her. Lack of courage and talk of us little people who can't do *anything* are signs of the lack of the Spirit.

Resistance against the arms producer who dominates us is coming today from many Christians. Many are coming to understand how our own lives are increasingly constricted and infringed upon. The clearest examples are those who are no longer able to maintain the same pace in life: the aged, the disabled, the foreigners, the homeless. If there are less people to care for the aged, that also means that those who care for them are occupied only with technical things—food, bedchanging, cleaning—and have no time for chatting with them or doing them a favor. We could put many more people to work in social areas where we need more nurses, teachers, social workers. There is plenty of work to do, but when weapons are the most important thing for a nation, then those other jobs, which create more employment possibilities, are forgotten.

For these reasons the struggle for peace is most important for us now: we all must discover what is happening in Germany because of the new nuclear bombs, whom they damage and who gains from them. Everyone, big or small, can become involved in this work of clarification. I know two boys who have taken it upon themselves to gather signatures for the Krefeld Appeal, in which demands are made that we withdraw from this decision to increase arms production. These boys wanted to convince their grandmother and an aged aunt in their village to sign the Krefeld Appeal. They thought carefully about what they were wearing and determined that long hair,

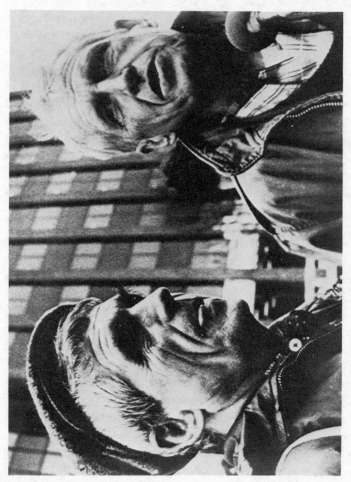

The Rev. Daniel Berrigan, S.J., and his brother, Philip Berrigan, members of the Plowshares Eight. (Religious News Service Photo)

faded jeans, and loud music do not make a very good impression. For the cause of peace, they told me with a grin, we can go once to the barber and put on some Sunday clothes. They prepared themselves intellectually for the discussion and tried to explain everything as precisely as possible so that their grandmother and aunt would not be outtalked by others who mouthed words about peace but really meant more rockets, more militarism, and more airport runways. This is a little story about how today swords are being beaten into plowshares:

> It will come to pass in the coming days: He shall establish what is right for the nations, and shall judge for many peoples. They shall beat their swords into plows and their instruments of murder into vineyard tools. Nation shall not make war against another, neither shall they train soldiers any more.
>
> Isaiah 2:2, 4 (Soelle-Steffensky)

> . . . and they shall beat their swords into plowshares, and their spears into pruning hooks; nation shall not lift up sword against nation, neither shall they learn war any more.
>
> Micah 4:3

More and more people "are not learning war any more," for they are refusing to learn how to wage war, they are declining military service.

Eight people belong to the American group called the Plowshares Eight: the Jesuit priest Daniel Berrigan, his brother Philip (who was also a Catholic priest), a housewife who is the mother of five children, an attorney, and others. Many of these people had already been at work in the resistance during the American war in Vietnam. For example, they burned the official orders of the soldiers with napalm, the poisonous substance the Americans used in Vietnam against the civilian population, or they poured blood over records at the military draft office. They follow the teaching of Christ and the theories which Mahatma Gandhi developed on nonviolent resistance. They understand nonviolence in the strictest sense: anything that hurts or damages another human being is for them unacceptable. But that does not mean that they respect all laws and hold property to be sacred. A sign in front of a weapons depot with the words "No Trespassing" is not binding for them. Daniel Berrigan says: "No weapon ever rusts or rots away without being used. No weapon, once it has been made, has ever prevented weapons from being multiplied and improved. No weapons system since the discovery of gunpowder has prevented the start of a war. No war, once it has started, has ever led to peace" (Public forum, 17 April 1981).

On 9 September 1980 these eight men and women entered a subsidiary agency of General Electric in the suburban community of King of Prussia, Pennsylvania. Nuclear missiles were being built in this factory. While one woman got a discussion going with the guard over the meaning of such instruments of murder, the others quickly rushed into the plant and with hammers destroyed two of the nuclear warheads (Mark 12a). They sprinkled human blood, their own, on classified construction plans. In their explanation of this act of "civil disobedience" they explained how General Electric receives three thousand dollars of tax money per day.

> . . . a monstrous robbery of the poor. These missiles increase the threat of nuclear war by their first-strike capability. This means that General Electric is working for the possible annihilation of millions of innocent lives.
> We have decided to obey God's law of life and not a contract to do business with death. If we of today are to beat our swords into plowshares, then we must try to make the biblical appeal concrete.

The Plowshares Eight have in the meantime been sentenced to prison for between two to ten years. But their example is catching on and has contributed a great deal to the fact that now an active peace movement has begun in the United States too.

People in this movement understand disobedience to laws as obedience to God. They hold the destruction of instruments of murder to be a just act.

There are many forms of this nonviolent resistance against the military's rule of force. A street or a railway used to transport poison or nuclear weapons can be blocked. Military installations can be occupied, and discussions begun with soldiers about what they are really doing. In Hanover young people have lain in front of the entrances to a weapons exhibit.

"Whoever walks over us walks over corpses as well," they said to the international weapons dealers. In Washington, D.C., resistance fighters have poured blood on the beautiful white marble columns. Such a nonviolent action, in which no one is injured, is called a *symbolic action*. This comes from the tradition of Mahatma Gandhi, who freed his country from the English colonialists. When Daniel Berrigan was asked why they utilize such symbols, he said:

> At the Pentagon we are dealing with the disabled, with the intellectually disabled. We are dealing with an irrational power. Therefore, we are using not only rational means of communication like flyers and conversations, but also a-rational ones, namely symbols. Symbols serving to concretize death. The generals never get to see the other side of their decisions. A deep gulf exists between decision making and its results. It is shocking to see human blood in the spotless corridors of the Pentagon. There is nothing more horrible for the people who are employed in this gigantic Greek temple. Suddenly the truth of our situation is out into the open and under our feet, and this is terrible.
>
> For us—for most of us are Christians—this is an extension of our regular worship of God. For us our tradition is sacred. It is full of symbol: human blood, ashes, water, oil.
>
> We look at it like this: We take the body and blood from the altar and bring it to the Pentagon. In the same way Christ was brought from the Last Supper to Golgotha, in one single day.

There are also forms of passive resistance against militarism which have been accomplished by Christians. The Catholic archbishop of Seattle, Raymond Hunthausen, refused to pay 50 percent of his taxes because this money is blood money to be used for preparation for war. He is prepared to answer for this action and go to prison. One of the fathers of this resistance movement was the American Henry Thoreau, who fought in the nineteenth century against slavery and the war against Mexico. He said: "Under a government which imprisons anyone unjustly, prison is the proper place for a just man . . . it is the only place in a slave state where a free man can dwell with honor."

A Christian group in Washington, D.C., the Sojourners, which lives in a slum and works together with the most poverty-stricken people compares our life today with the period of slavery in the nineteenth century. Nuclear arms proliferation, they say, is like slavery. It is unjust, oppression, exploitation. It is a crime against the poor. Whoever tolerates this crime shares the guilt of it.

In the previous century many said: There always have been slaves. It is an economic necessity. We can't change that.

Today many say: There have always been wars. Nuclear arms are politically necessary. We can't change that.

But just as when slavery was abolished—because more and more people, among them many Christians, found it unacceptable to live in a slave state—so today more and more people are finding it unacceptable to live in a nuclear state.

God has disarmed unilaterally. He has come out on the side of the poor. In Jesus he has demonstrated a different way of living together, free of exerting violence against and pressure upon others. We cannot speak of God's love as long as we continue to produce weapons. We cannot seek God's righteousness and justice if we continue to participate in the greatest crime of humanity. And we cannot be human ourselves as long as we allow just anything to be done with us.